THE MOVIE GAME

THE
MOVIE
GAME

BY
Tony DiMarco
&
Tod Faulkner

Panoply Publications
LOS ANGELES, CALIFORNIA

ISBN 13:
978-0-981 8391-4-1

ISBN 10:
0-981 8391-4-2

Published and bound in the United States of America

Dedicated to movie buffs everywhere,
past, present and future.

Contents

Preface

Movies are our world's most unifying force — a popular spectrum of reference for most people on earth. Although they don't much care who won this year's World Series, folks from Bangalore, India to Brisbane, Australia will argue passionately, angrily, fervently about who deserves this year's Oscar for Best Supporting Actress.

Whatever else they think about us, people in almost every country on earth love and are culturally influenced by our movies. For more than 100 years, American movies have been the most common mutual topic of our planet — from Mary Pickford to Daniel Day Lewis, from D. W. Griffith's "Birth of a Nation" to Alejandro G. Inarritu's "The Revenant," from small, single camera black and white movies to the huge special effects-laden powerhouse films of this generation.

Given all that, nothing brings these billions of movie fans more social pleasure than talking about the movies, quizzing each other to see who knows the most, friends trying to stump friends. Movie knowledge almost always gets competitive, and, dragging that point to its next obvious station, isn't it time someone created a quiz show about the movies — about all those actors and actresses, all those stories and spectacular effects, and all the rest of it?

Yep, it's time.

"The Movie Game" is a people-pleasing programming idea whose time has come. This program will welcome celebrity and civilian contestants before the cameras to show off and win money with their knowledge of Hollywood's movies, its actors, actresses, directors and all the other people and events connected with the world's most exciting industry.

This book is an adjunct to the game and, in fact, the most important element of the whole project. Here are the typical questions that make the game run, the trivia that makes up the joy of competition unleashed by the game itself. This book, if you will, gives the reader a chance to do the homework necessary to be an official expert film buff. Or, on the other hand, it can function as good reading material for anyone with an interest in motion pictures. So, you can sit back and put your movie trivia skills to the test or just read the questions and answers and, perhaps, learn some things you never knew about the vast world of motion pictures.

The questions range from those that are fairly simple to some that are, admittedly, very difficult. The answer is in small print just below the question. It's up to you whether you want to peek before you're sure of the answer or if you want to try to get the answer before checking to see if it's correct. In any event, enjoy the quiz and let the questions begin!

Actors

1) Which one of the following athletes did Ronald Reagan *not* portray in a movie?
a) Christy Mathewson b) Grover Cleveland Alexander c) George Gipp
ANS. A

2) Fredric March, Spencer Tracy and John Barrymore all played the lead role in versions of "Dr. Jekyll and Mr. Hyde." Who was first?
ANS: BARRYMORE IN 1920; MARCH (1931); TRACY (1941).

3) Through 2017, Denzel Washington has won two acting Oscars. What differentiates the two?
ANS: ONE WAS FOR BEST ACTOR ("TRAINING DAY" IN 2002), THE OTHER WAS FOR BEST SUPPORTING ACTOR ("GLORY" IN 1990).

4) Entertainment Weekly voted him the 22nd greatest movie star of all time even though he only appeared in only three major film roles.
ANS: JAMES DEAN.

SPENCER TRACY

CARY GRANT

5) He said this about his co-star, Marilyn Monroe: "Marilyn was an incredible person to act with, the most marvelous I ever worked with and I have been working for 29 years."
a) Tom Ewell b) Tony Curtis
c) Montgomery Clift d) Jack Lemmon
ANS: C

6) Gregory Peck played Capt. Ahab in the 1956 version of "Moby Dick." Who played the ill-fated captain in the 1926 version of the story?
a) John Barrymore b) Douglas Fairbanks Sr.
c) Ramon Navarro d) John Gilbert
ANS: A

7) How old was Orson Welles when he wrote, directed and starred in "Citizen Kane?"
a) 28 b) 30 c) 25 d) 22
ANS: C

8) William Powell's classmate at Central High School in Kansas City, Missouri, became a famous baseball icon. Who was he?
a) Leo Durocher b) Casey Stengel c) Branch Rickey
d) Tommy Lasorda
ANS: B

JAMES DEAN

9) Which one of these leading men did not appear opposite

Doris Day in one of her films?
a) Clark Gable b) Jack Lemmon c) Gene Kelly
d) Cary Grant
ANS. C

10) Herbert Lom (1962), Claude Rains (1943), Lon Chaney Sr. (1925) and Gerard Butler (2004) all played the title role in different versions of what film?
ANS: "THE PHANTOM OF THE OPERA."

11) True or False: George Clooney's aunt was singer Rosemary Clooney.
ANS: TRUE. GEORGE'S FATHER IS TV NEWSMAN, NICK, ROSEMARY'S BROTHER.

12) After a sensational debut on television as an alien from outer-space, he portrayed the iconic cartoon character, "Popeye" in his first movie. Who was he?
ANS: ROBIN WILLIAMS.

13) Russell Crowe starred in the remake of "3:10 to

CLARK GABLE   GARY COOPER

FREDRIC MARCH

Yuma." Who played Crowe's role in the original film?
ANS: GLENN FORD.

14) Who played Jimmy Bond, James Bond's nephew, in the 1967 version of "Casino Royale?"
a) Woody Allen b) Mickey Rooney c) Jack Lemmon d) Robert Downey Jr.
ANS: A

15) The middle name of Leonardo Di Caprio, who is partly of German descent, is:
a) Wilhelm b) Hans c) Franz d) Rudolph
ANS: A

16) Orlando Bloom has appeared in the sequels to what movies?
ANS: "THE LORD OF THE RINGS" AND "PIRATES OF THE CARIBBEAN."

17) Marlon Brando was how old when he played Don Vito Corleone in "The Godfather?"
a) 52 b) 48 c) 60 d) 44
ANS: B

18) Johnny Depp says which of his movies was his first "proper" film?
a) "Edward Scissorshands"
b) "Ed Wood" c) "Platoon"
ANS: C

GREGORY PECK

19) Robert Mitchum was the

villain in the 1962 version of "Cape Fear." Who played the Mitchum role in the 1991 version of the film?

ANS: ROBERT DE NIRO.

20) Gary Cooper played real-life characters such as Lou Gehrig, Sgt. Alvin York, and Gen. Billy Mitchell. Name one more that he also portrayed.

ANS: MARCO POLO, WILD BILL HICKOK OR DR. WASSELL.

MONTGOMERY CLIFT

21) He was a popular actor in the 1930s, played the harassed producer/director in "42nd Street" and was the original "Cisco Kid." Name him.
a) Warren William b) Warner Baxter c) Philip Reed d) John Boles

ANS: B

CHARLES BRONSON

ERNEST BORGNINE

22) Tom Cruise was how old when he made his film debut?
a) 17 b) 22 c) 19 d) 20
ANS: C

23) Before he became Fred Mertz in "I Love Lucy" he appeared mostly as a gruff but amiable character in more than 100 films. Who was he?
ANS: WILLIAM FRAWLEY.

JOHN BARRYMORE

24) In what film did Spencer Tracy and Fredric March co-star?
ANS: "INHERIT THE WIND," 1960.

25) This actor was a member of the rock band, "Kids."
a) Johnny Depp b) Leonardo Di Caprio c) Tom Cruise d) Orlando Bloom
ANS: A

ERROL FLYNN

26) Donald O'Connor played the role of Peter Stirling in seven of eight "Francis the Talking Mule" films. Who played the role in the eighth film?
ANS: MICKEY ROONEY.

27) As a former circus performer, he would stay in shape by working out on the high bar.
a) Tony Curtis b) Charles Bronson c) Burt Lancaster

d) Lee Marvin
ANS: C

28) "Stagecoach" was one of six films John Wayne made in 1939 but is considered his break-through film. What film did he make immediately after "Stagecoach?"
a) "Allegheny Uprising" b) "Three Texas Steers" c) "Night Riders" d) "Wyoming Outlaw"
ANS: C

JOHN WAYNE

29) Of the following actors who played the Frankenstein monster, who played him first?
a) Lon Chaney Sr. b) Boris Karloff c) Charles Ogle d) Owen Moore
ANS: C, CHARLES OGLE IN 1910.

30) George Clooney wore another hat besides "actor" in "Leatherheads." What was it?
ANS: HE DIRECTED THE FILM.

CHARLTON HESTON

31) Name three actors who have played Fletcher Christian in different versions of "Mutiny on the Bounty."
a) Clark Gable, Cary Grant and Mel Gibson b) Franchot Tone, Charles Laughlin and Marlon Brando c) Clark Gable, Mel Gibson and Marlon Brando
ANS: C

CHRISTIAN BALE

32) Who played Robert DeNiro's son in "This Boy's Life?"
ANS: LEONARDO DI CAPRIO.

33) Gregory Peck is credited with being the star of his very first film. What was it?
a) "The Keys to the Kingdom"
b) "Days of Glory" c) "Spellbound" d) "The Valley of Decision"
ANS: B (IN 1944.)

34) Clark Gable appeared in the original and in the same role in the remake of what film?
ANS: "RED DUST" (1932) REMADE AS "MOGAMBO" IN 1953.

35 Jack Lemmon and Tony Curtis had the male leads in "Some Like It Hot," but three of the supporting actors were leading men in the 1930s. Can you name them?
ANS: GEORGE RAFT, PAT O'BRIEN AND JOE E. BROWN.

CRAIG STEVENS

36) Cary Grant played opposite many leading ladies during his career. But not with one of the below:
a) Priscilla Lane b) Leslie Caron c) Claudette Colbert d) Sophia Loren
ANS: C

37) Who was the actor who played Moses in "The History of the World, Part 1?"

ANS: MEL BROOKS.

38) These stars became famous for their television roles. One did not go on to fame in movies.
a) James Garner b) Robin Williams c) Tom Hanks
d) Jerry Seinfeld
ANS: D

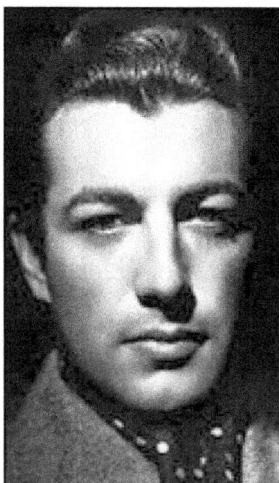

ROBERT TAYLOR

39) John Wayne made his last movie, "The Shootist," in 1976. What year did he appear in his first film?
a) 1926 b) 1932 c) 1938 d) 1929
ANS: A

40) At 6"4" John Wayne had good size. Did he ever play college football?
ANS: YES, BUT INJURIES CUT HIS CAREER SHORT AT USC.

41) Craig Stevens reprised his popular TV role as the suave private eye, Peter Gunn, for a 1967 movie. What was its title?
a) "Peter Gunn" b) "Gunn for Hire" c) "Gunn"
d) "This Gun for Hire"
ANS: C

42) What soon to be superstar portrayed the villain in the 1936 film, "After the Thin Man?"
a) Robert Taylor b) Robert Mitchum c) James Stewart d) Tyrone Power
ANS: C

43) George Sanders, usually cast as a smooth villain, had one singing role in which he displayed an excellent baritone voice. What was the movie?

ANS: "CALL ME MADAM," 1953, IN THE ROLE OF GEN. COSMO CONSTANTINE.

44) Robert Taylor was 25 when he played opposite Greta Garbo in the 1936 film, "Camille." How old was Garbo?
a) 21 b) 31 c) 27 d) 24
ANS: B

TOM HANKS

45) This actor spelled his real last name backwards to get his stage name. Can you name him?
ANS: HOWARD KEEL, WHOSE REAL LAST NAME WAS LEEK.

46) Francis, the star of eight Universal films, was a "talking"...?
a) Mule b) Horse c) Dog d) Cat
ANS: A

ROBIN WILLIAMS

47) The media has dubbed him "Mr. July" because most of his blockbuster movies have opened in July.
a) Tom Cruise b) James Franco c) Will Smith d) Ben Affleck
ANS: C

48) He started acting with Jr. after his name because his father was an actor with the same name.
a) Robert Taylor b) Tyrone Power c) William Powell

JAMES STEWART

d) James Stewart
ANS: B

49) Who is the tallest of the following actors?
a) James Stewart b) Walter Matthau c) Clint Eastwood d) Tom Selleck
ANS: EASTWOOD AT 6'4". STEWART WAS 6'3 1/2", MATTHAU 6'2 1/2", SELLECK 6'3 1/2".

50) Who said "I'm no actor and I have 64 pictures to prove it?"
a) Humphrey Bogart b) Victor Mature c) Stirling Hayden d) Tony Curtis
ANS: B

51) Tom Selleck played a baseball pitcher in "Mr. Baseball." What sport did he participate in at college?
ANS: BASKETBALL. HE WAS A RESERVE FOR USC.

52) More height questions. Who is the tallest among: Tom Cruise, Alan Ladd, James Cagney, Humphrey Bogart and Dustin Hoffman?
ANS: BOGART WAS 5'8", CRUISE IS 5'7", CAGNEY, 5'6 1/2", LADD, 5'6 1/4," AND HOFFMAN, 5'5 3/4".

DAVID NIVEN

53) When George Raft said he didn't want to "star opposite an unknown Swedish broad," what film and what actress was he referring to?
ANS: "CASABLANCA" AND INGRID

SEAN CONNERY

BERGMAN.

54) What actor, when he briefly retired, said, "You can only hold your stomach in for so many years."
a) Sean Connery b) Roger Moore) c) Burt Reynolds d) Richard Burton
ANS C

55) Who said, "You can tell a lot about a fellow's character by his way of eating jelly-beans?"
a) James Cagney b) George Clooney c) Ronald Reagan d) Tom Hanks
ANS: C

56) Who said "Everybody wants to be Cary Grant. Even I want to be Cary Grant."
ANS: CARY GRANT.

57) What actor said "Know your lines and don't bump into the furniture?"
a) Humphrey Bogart b) James Cagney c) Frank Sinatra d) Spencer Tracy
ANS: D

BRAD PITT

58) In 1958, Louis Jourdan played the role of Gaston Lachaille opposite Leslie Caron in "Gigi." Jourdan later appeared in the stage version of the movie. What role did he

BEN AFFLECK

play?

ANS: THE ROLE OF GASTON'S UNCLE, HONORE, PLAYED BY MAURICE CHEVALIER IN THE FILM.

59) Which of the following actors did not play Frankenstein's monster in a movie?
a) Lon Chaney Sr. b) Glenn Strange c) Robert DeNiro d) Christopher Lee
ANS: A

60) Suave Basil Rathbone oftentimes was cast as a villain but he played what private eye in a series of films?
ANS: SHERLOCK HOLMES.

61) Clint Eastwood appeared in the 1955 film, "Francis in the Navy." Who was the star of the film?
ANS: DONALD O'CONNOR.

62) He was more famous after he starred in the lead role of "Kojak" on television, but he was the Bond villain in "On Her Majesty's Secret Service." What was his name?
ANS: TELLY SAVALAS.

63) Cary Grant starred with actresses ranging from Shirley Temple to Mae West. Which one of the following did he not appear with?
a) Sophia Loren b) Doris Day

DWAYNE JOHNSON

DAN BLOCKER

c) Myrna Loy d) Lauren Bacall
ANS: D

64) What actor played the title role in the first James Bond film, "Dr. No?"
a) Christopher Lee b) Peter Cushing c) Joseph Wiseman d) Robert Shaw
ANS: C

65) In addition to each being an actor and leading man, what do these stars also have in common: Spencer Tracy, Frank Sinatra, Pat O'Brien and Bing Crosby?
ANS: ALL PLAYED A CATHOLIC PRIEST IN ONE OR MORE MOVIES.

66) One of these actors did not play James Bond in a movie:
a) Timothy Dalton b) David Niven c) Pierce Brosnan d) Richard Burton.
ANS: D

LORNE GREENE

67) What is the relationship between Ben and Casey Affleck?
ANS: THEY ARE BROTHERS.

68) Louis Jourdan was a Bond villain long after co-starring in the 1958 Academy Award winning, "Gigi." What Bond film was he in?
ANS: "OCTOPUSSY" IN 1983.

69) Michael Landon starred in

three television series but made an auspicious debut in what motion picture?
ANS: HE WAS THE STAR OF "I WAS A TEENAGE WEREWOLF." (1957)

70) All these movie stars but one crossed over into television with shows named for them. Who was the lone holdout?
a) Fred Astaire b) Doris Day c) James Stewart d) Dick Powell e) Cary Grant
ANS: E

GEORGE SANDERS

71) Which of the following TV series stars was considered for a lead role in the motion picture, "MASH?"
a) Richard Crenna b) Dan Blocker c) George Maharis d) Robert Vaughn
ANS: B

GEORGE RAFT

72) Name another actor besides Ronald Reagan who rose to a high, national political office from California.
ANS: GEORGE MURPHY WAS U. S. SENATOR FROM CALIFORNIA FROM 1965 TO 1971.

73) Rossano Brazzi played the role of Emile de Beque in the film version of "South Pacific," but his singing voice was dubbed by a popular Metropolitan Opera baritone. Who was he?

WILL SMITH

a) Ezio Pinza b) Sherrill Milnes c) Giorgio Tozzi d) Tito Gobi
ANS: C

74) Lorne Greene is best known as the patriarch Ben Cartwright in the popular "Bonanza" series. What role did he play in the film, "Peyton Place?"
a) A doctor b) A corporate executive c) A lawyer d) A police lieutenant
ANS: C

75) What actor wanted to change the name of his street in Beverly Hills to "Rue de Vallee?"
ANS: RUDY VALLLEE.

76) Cary Grant and Shirley Temple co-starred in what film?
ANS: "THE BACHELOR AND THE BOBBY SOXER" IN 1947.

77) What pair of the following are not siblings?
a) George Sanders and Tom Conway b) Dana Andrews and Steve Forrest c) Sean and MacKenzie Astin d) William and Dick Powell
ANS: D

78) Speaking of siblings, these stars numbered not two, but three. Who were they?
ANS: JOHN, LIONEL AND ETHEL BARRYMORE.

STEVE MC QUEEN

TOM CRUISE   RUSSELL CROWE

79) What actor had the lead in an Alfred Hitchcock thriller before he gained fame in a film that was the first of a popular series.
ANS: SEAN CONNERY IN "MARNIE."

80) He played a rather slick villain in "Charade" but he became forever popular for his comedy roles, many with Jack Lemmon.
ANS: WALTER MATTHAU.

81) Which of these actors did not play Abraham Lincoln in a movie?
a) Daniel Day-Lewis b) Raymond Massey c) Henry Fonda d) Charlton Heston
ANS: D

82) Why was the telephone sometimes referred to as "The Ameche" in the late 1930s and 1940s?
ANS: BECAUSE DON AMECHE PLAYED THE INVENTOR OF THE TELEPHONE IN THE 1939 MOVIE, "THE STORY OF ALEXANDER GRAHAM BELL."

ORLANDO BLOOM

83) Famed acting instructor Lee Strasberg made one of his rare acting appearances as Hyman Roth in what film?
ANS: "THE GODFATHER, PART 2."

84) One of these actors did not play Al Capone in a movie.
a) Robert DeNiro b) Edward G. Robinson c) Ben Gazzara d) Rod Steiger
ANS: B

85) Who played future president Franklin Delano Roosevelt in "Sunrise at Campobello?"
ANS: RALPH BELLAMY.

86) Which one of these actors did not play composer Cole Porter in a motion picture?
a) Tyrone Power b) Kevin Kline c) Cary Grant
ANS: A

JAMES CAGNEY

87) Spencer Tracy played the adult Thomas Edison in "Edison the Man." Who played "Young Thomas Edison?"
ANS: MICKEY ROONEY.

88) Charlton Heston played many historical characters. Which one of the following did he not play?
a) John the Baptist b) Marc Antony c) Alexander the Great d) Michelangelo
ANS: C

RAY MILLAND

89) At 6'4" it wasn't easy for Howard Keel to find a tall leading lady for his musicals. Which of the following was the tallest and the shortest of his musical co-stars?
a) Jane Powell b) Esther Williams c) Doris Day d) Betty Hutton e) Kathryn Grayson
ANS: TALLEST, B), ESTHER WILLIAMS AT 5'8 1/2". SHORTEST, A), JANE POWELL, AT 5'1".

90) James Stewart made four films that were directed by Alfred Hitchcock. What were the films?
ANS: "ROPE," 1948; "REAR WINDOW," 1954; "THE MAN WHO KNEW TOO MUCH," 1956 AND "VERTIGO," 1958.

91) Among his many film roles, Pat O'Brien is remembered for portraying Notre Dame football coach Knute Rockne. Name another real life football coach played by O'Brien.
ANS: FRANK CAVANAUGH OF FORDHAM IN "THE IRON MAJOR," 1943.

92) What actor played Benito Juarez, Louis Pasteur and Emile Zola in biopics of these historical personalities?
a) Edward G. Robinson b) Raymond Massey c) Paul Muni
d) George Raft
ANS: C

DENZEL WASHINGTON

93) Who said that seeing James Cagney's portrayal of George M. Cohan made it seem like it was the real Cohan on

ROBERT MITCHUM

the screen?
a) Cohan's daughter b) Cohan's wife c) Cohan's manager d) Cohan's parents
ANS: B

94) What future president did Cliff Robertson portray in "PT-109?"
ANS: JOHN F. KENNEDY.

95) "The Red Tent," in which Sean Connery played explorer Roald Amundson, was made by a film company from what country?
a) England b) Italy c) Russia d) Germany
ANS: C

96 Which of these actors did not play Capt. Bligh in a movie based on the mutiny on The Bounty?
a) Anthony Hopkins b) Charles Laughton c) Trevor Howard d) Alec Guiness
ANS: D

97) According to Forbes Magazine, the highest paid actor for 2016, at $64.5 million, was:
a) Matt Damon b) Vin Diesel
c) Jennifer Lawrence
d) Dwayne Johnson
ANS: D

98) Gregory Peck usually played heroes, but in this film he was a pretty nasty character.

ORSON WELLES

a) "Arabesque" b) "The Boys from Brazil" c) "The Chairman" d) "Designing Woman"
ANS: B

99) Who played Richard Burton's father in "Alexander the Great?"
a) Fredric March b) Trevor Howard c) Charlton Heston d) Orson Welles
ANS: A

FRANK SINATRA

100) Richard Harris and Vanessa Redgrave essayed the lead roles in the movie version of "Camelot." Who played them on Broadway?
ANS: RICHARD BURTON AND JULIE ANDREWS.

101) Matt Damon has appeared in two different sequel franchises. What are they?
ANS: THE "BOURNE" AND THE "OCEANS" FILMS.

102) What actors have played former President Richard Nixon in films?
ANS: ANTHONY HOPKINS AND FRANK LANGELLA.

103) Who played the Henry Higgins role in "Pygmalion?"
ANS: LESLIE HOWARD.

104first talking movie?
a) "The Plainsman" b) "The Virginian" c) "Arizona Bound" d) "Wings"
ANS: C

HOWARD KEEL

JACK LEMMON   TONY CURTIS

105) Who was Herman Mankiewicz referring to when he said, "There, but for the grace of God, goes God."

ANS: ORSON WELLES.

106 About what actor was the following said: "He takes his place beside children and animals as one of the great scene stealers of all time."
a) Spencer Tracy b) Maurice Chevalier c) Marlon Brando d) Jimmy Durante
ANS: B

107) What actor said, "Movies bore me. Especially my own."
a) Humphrey Bogart b) Spencer Tracy c) Robert Mitchum d) Richard Burton
ANS: C

108) He was rescued during World War I, came to Hollywood and became one of the most popular actors of the 1920s. Legend has it he was nominated for a Best Actor Oscar but was disqualified because he was a dog. What was his name?

GORDON MACRAE

a) Rin Tin Tin b) Asta c) Toto
d) Benji
ANS: A

109) Who played the Wizard in
the 1939 version of "The Wizard of Oz?"
ANS: VETERAN CHARACTER ACTOR
FRANK MORGAN.

110) These actors all made
their screen debuts in what
year? Ava Gardner, Charlton
Heston, Frank Sinatra, Cyd
Charisse.
a) 1946 b) 1941 c) 1939
d) 1950
ANS: B

111) Fred Astaire's dancing partner prior to Ginger
Rogers was his sister. What was her first name?
a) Iris b) Adele c) Sally d) Alice
ANS: B

112) Who did Abe Vigoda play
in "Godfather I" and "Godfather II?"
a) Barzini b) Luca Brazzi
c) Fredo d) Tessio
ANS: D

113) Mark Harmon's father
was an all-America football
player at the University of
Michigan who played himself
in his movie biography. Who
was he?
ANS: TOM HARMON.

GEORGE CLOONEY

LEONARDO
DI CAPRIO

114) Jack Lemmon and Tony Curtis made one other film together besides "Some Like It Hot" in 1959. What was it?
ANS: "THE GREAT RACE" IN 1965.

115) What was the first movie in which Peter Sellers portrayed Inspector Clouseau?
ANS: "A SHOT IN THE DARK."

116) Which one of these actors did not play Sam Spade in the movies?
a) Ricardo Cortez b) Howard Duff c) Humphrey Bogart d) Warren William
ANS: B. HOWARD DUFF. DUFF PLAYED SPADE ON THE RADIO, BUT NOT IN A FILM.

117) Who is the only actor to play Batman more than twice?
ANS: CHRISTIAN BALE.

118) Three of these actors played Charlie Chan in different films. Who who did not?
a) Warner Oland b) Peter Lorre c) Roland Winters d) Sidney Toler
ANS: B

119) Who played King Kaiser, a take-off of Sid Caesar, in "My Favorite Year?"
a) Joseph Bologna b) Richard Conte c) Joe Mantegna d) Alan Alda
ANS: A

TYRONE POWER

WILLIAM HOLDEN

120) What are the names of Lloyd Bridges' actor-sons?
ANS: BEAU AND JEFF.

121) Jack Lemmon was an alumnus of what university?
a) New York University
b) Harvard c) Indiana
d) Boston College
ANS: B

122) Who was the smooth-talking voice of Shere Kahn the Tiger in Disney's animated version of "The Jungle Book?"
ANS: GEORGE SANDERS.

123) What events have caused Jack Nicholson to alter his movie-making schedule?
ANS: L. A. LAKERS HOME BASKETBALL GAMES.

124 The most popular male star of the 1990s was:
a) Arnold Schwarzenegger b) Will Smith c) Tom Cruise d) Tom Hanks
ANS: C

125 Who originated Ernest Borgnine's Academy Award winning role of "Marty" in the television version that pre-ceded the film?
a) Jack Palance b) Rod Steiger c) Eli Wallach d) Charles Bronson
ANS: B

BURT LANCASTER

CHARLES BOYER

126) He was strongly considered for the role of Jack Dawson, which was played by Leonardo DiCaprio, in "Titanic" (1997).
a) Matthew McConaughey
b) Ben Affleck c) Brad Pitt
d) Johnny Depp
ANS: A

127) True or False: Actor Russell Crowe was born in Australia.
ANS: FALSE. HE WAS BORN IN NEW ZEALAND, RAISED IN AUSTRALIA.

128) He went from playing crooners in 1930s musicals to a hard-boiled private eye in the 1940s. Who was he?
a) Frank Sinatra b) Bing Crosby c) Dick Powell
d) Gordon MacRae
ANS: C

129) Who played Tonto in the 2013 version of "The Lone Ranger?"
a) Johnny Depp b) Ben Affleck
c) George Clooney d) Brad Pitt
ANS: A

130) Zero Mostel was the original Tevye in the Broadway production of "Fiddler on the Roof." Who played the role in the movie version?
a) Howard Keel b) Zero Mostel
c) Herschel Bernardi d) Topol
ANS: D

LOUIS JOURDAN

131) The 1964 movie, "Zulu," was the break-through film for what English actor?
a) Roger Moore b) Stanley Baker c) Michael Caine d) Jack Hawkins
ANS: C

132) He, along with Eddie Murphy, is one of two African-Americans in the list of the top five highest grossing actors of all time.
a) Sidney Poitier b) Denzel Washington c) Harry Belafonte d) Morgan Freeman
ANS: D

WILLIAM POWELL

133) He was a world-class bridge player and was known to postpone shootings so he could attend bridge matches.
ANS: OMAR SHARIF.

DICK POWELL

134) Fred Astaire heard him singing and got him an agent and he appeared in several early Warner Bros. musicals. But he spent most of his career as a straight actor and not in musicals.
a) Pat O'Brien b) Dana Andrews c) Walter Pidgeon d) George Raft
ANS: C

135) Vincent Price said his all-time favorite actor was?

a) James Stewart b) Richard Burton c) Marlon Brando d) Cary Grant
ANS: D

136) He was the best man at the 1952 wedding of Ronald Reagan and Nancy Davis.
a) William Holden b) Pat O'Brien c) James Cagney d) Bob Hope
ANS: A

FRED ASTAIRE

137) He went from motion picture leading man to television sidekick and had a California state park named after him. Who was he?
a) Lon Chaney b) Joe E. Brown c) Leo Carrillo d) Caesar Romero
ANS: C

138) One of these actors did not play Billy the Kid.
a) Paul Newman b) Roy Rogers c) Emilio Estevez d) Tony Curtis
ANS: D

139) He is the only U. S. Senator represented by a star on the Hollywood Walk of Fame.
ANS: GEORGE MURPHY.

140) At least 10 versions of "The Prisoner of Zenda" have been made, dating back to 1913. Which one of these actors did not star in one of the versions?
a) Peter Sellers b) Ronald Colman c) Stewart Granger

WALTER PIDGEON

d) John Barrymore
ANS: D

141) Jose Ferrar and Gerard Depardieu played the title role in the 1950 and 1990 versions of "Cyrano de Bergerac." What actor played the lead in "Roxanne," which was based on the Cyrano story?
a) Chevy Chase b) Jack Lemmon c) Steve Martin
d) Jerry Lewis
ANS: C

GEORGE MURPHY

142) These two actors, with similar sounding last names, have appeared in movie versions of "Superman." Name them.
ANS: GEORGE REEVES AND CHRISTOPHER REEVE.

RONALD COLMAN AND MADELEINE CARROLL IN THE 1937 VERSION OF "THE PRISONER OF ZENDA."

HENRY FONDA

143) How many Matt Helm movies did Dean Martin make between 1966 and 1968?
a) 3 b) 5) c) 4 d) 2
ANS: C

144) Erich von Stroheim, who directed and acted in many silent films and played Gloria Swanson's ("Norma Desmond") servant in "Sunset Boulevard," was called:
ANS: "THE MAN YOU LOVE TO HATE."

145) Who starred as Harry Palmer is three films between 1965 and 1967?
a) Michael Caine b) Richard Burton c) Richard Harris d) Stanley Baker
ANS: A

146) Who was called "The First Gentleman of the Screen?"
a) Laurence Olivier b) George Arliss c) Paul Muni d) Edward G. Robinson
ANS: B

147) Bing Crosby played Father Chuck O'Malley in the films, "Going My Way" and "The Bells of St. Mary's." Who played Fr. O'Malley in the television version of "Going My Way?" (1962).
ANS: GENE KELLY.

WALTER HUSTON

148) Wyatt Earp has been portrayed in movies by such actors as James Stewart, Burt Lancaster, Kurt Russell, Walter Huston, James Garner and Joel McCrea, among others. Who played him first?
ANS: WALTER HUSTON IN "LAW AND ORDER" IN 1932.

149) Who was the actor who played Dr. Kildare in the first film made with that character?
a) Lew Ayres b) Joel McCrea
c) Richard Chamberlain
d) Mark Jenkins
ANS: B

MICHAEL CAINE

150) Several actors played The Cisco Kid in the series that was made between 1929 and 1950. Who portrayed the Kid the most times?
a) Warner Baxter b) Cesar Romero c) Duncan Renaldo d) Gilbert Roland
ANS: C (8 TIMES).

151) Jeff Chandler played what Indian warrior in three films?
a) Cochise b) Sitting Bull
c) Geronimo d) Tonto
ANS: A

152) There were 13 films made about detective Boston Blackie. Who played the lead in these?
a) Sam Levene b) Chester

ERICH von STROHEIM

SIDNEY
GREENSTREET

Morris c) Lee J. Cobb
d) Robert Paige
ANS: B

153) Bulldog Drummond has been portrayed by several different actors. One of the following did not play Drummond.
a) Walter Pidgeon b) William Powell c) Ray Milland
d) Ralph Richardson
ANS: B

154) Sydney Greenstreet made his movie debut in 1941 in what film?
a) "The Maltese Falcon" b) "Casablanca" c) "Across the Pacific" d) "Background to Danger"
ANS: A

155 "Up the River" in 1930, with Humphrey Bogart, was notable as the screen debut of what actor?
a) Clark Gable b) James Stewart c) Spencer Tracy d) Robert Montgomery
ANS: C

156) Who turned down the lead in these four Humphrey Bogart films: "Dead End," "High Sierra," "The Maltese Falcon" and "Casablanca."
a) Edward G. Robinson b) George Raft c) Errol Flynn
d) Douglas Fairbanks Jr.
ANS: B

MATT DAMON

157) He was an all-America halfback at Alabama, was inducted into the College Football Hall of Fame and had an acting career that ran from 1927 to 1965. Name him.
ANS: JOHNNY MACK BROWN.

158) "The Mighty Barnum," the story of P. T. Barnum, released in 1934, starred what actor in the title role?
a) Edward Arnold b) Antonio Moreno c) Wallace Berry d) Frank Morgan
ANS: C

159) The first actor to star in a film as Robin Hood was:
a) Errol Flynn b) Douglas Fairbanks Sr. c) Rudolph Valentino d) Robert Clarke
ANS: B

160) Theodore Roosevelt was portrayed by Brian Keith in "The Wind and the Lion" (1976). Who portrayed Theodore Roosevelt Jr. in "The Longest

DANA ANDREWS   STEVE FOREST

MICHAEL KEATON

Day?" (1962).
ANS: HENRY FONDA.

161) Louis Hayward played The Saint in a 1938 and 1954 film. What actor played the character in five movies?
a) George Sanders b) Tom Conway c) Vincent Price d) Brian Aherne
ANS: A

162) Who played Sam Spade Jr., son of the famous San Francisco private eye, in the 1975 film, "The Black Bird?"
a) George Segal b) Woody Allen c) Tom Hanks d) Robert Cummings
ANS: A

163) In the 1974 movie, "Undercover Hero," he played nine roles. Who was he?
a) Alec Guiness b) Peter Sellers c) John Gielgud d) Vincent Price
ANS: B

164) Michael Keaton played the title role of Ray Kroc in "The Founder," 2016. What did Kroc found?
a) Wendy's b) Mc Donald's c) Starbuck's d) Apple
ANS: B

165) True or False: Actors Dana Andrews and Steve Forrest were cousins.
ANS: FALSE. THEY WERE BROTHERS.

OMAR SHARIF

Actresses

1) She was the highest paid woman in America in 1942. Who was she?
a) Bette Davis b) Katharine Hepburn c) Eleanor Roosevelt d) Mary Pickford
ANS: A

2) When asked if she really had anything on in her famous calendar photo, Marilyn Monroe replied:
ANS: "I HAD THE RADIO ON."

3) Lucille Ball and this actress were classmates in drama school.
a) Joan Crawford b) Joan Fontaine c) Bette Davis
d) Miriam Hopkins
ANS: C

4) Dolly Parton's co-star in "Rhinestone" was:
a) Kevin Kline b) Sylvester Stallone c) Dabney Coleman
d) Chevy Chase
ANS: B

KATHARINE HEPBURN

5) What actresses parents both won Academy Awards?
ANS: LIZA MINELLI (HER PARENTS WERE VINCENT MINELLI AND JUDY GARLAND).

6) How many films did Joanne Woodward appear in with her husband, Paul Newman?
a) 4 b) 12 c) 7 d) 10
ANS: D

7) Which of the acting sisters, Joan Fontaine and Olivia de Havilland, gave up her real last name and took on a stage name?

MERYL STREEP

ANS: JOAN FONTAINE. HER REAL NAME WAS JOAN DE HAVILLAND.

8) Bette Davis made more than 100 movies during her career. How many did she make in1932?
a) 5 b) 10 c) 8 d) 3
ANS: C

9) What actress said, "Everything you see I owe to spaghetti."
a) Gina Lollobrigida b) Sophia Loren c) Claudia Cardinale d) Anna Magnani
ANS: B

10) Who said "I'd rather be smart than a movie star."
a) Natalie Portman b) Zsa Zsa Gabor c) Madonna d) Mae West

VERONICA LAKE

BETTE DAVIS

ANS: A

11) Jane Peters isn't a bad stage name but this actress didn't use it even though it was her real name. Who was she?
a) Frances Farmer b) Carole Lombard c) Joan Crawford d) Joan Blondell
ANS: B

12) She was let go from the cast of "West Side Story" because she was too young.
a) Stefanie Powers b) Shirley Temple c) Jill St. John d) Ann-Margaret
ANS: STEFANIE POWERS. SHE WAS 15.

13) Mary Martin originated the role of Nellie Forbush in the stage version of "South Pacific." Who played the role in the movie version?
ANS: MITZI GAYNOR.

14) These two beauties Anglicized their Latina names from Raquel Tejada and Margarita Cansino to what?
ANS: RAQUEL WELCH AND RITA HAYWORTH.

15) Julia Childs was six feet tall. Who played her in a movie and what was her height?
ANS: MERYL STREEP, WHO IS 5'6" TALL.

INGRID BERGMAN

•45•

RAQUEL WELCH

16) Who is the shortest among these actresses?
a) Veronica Lake b) Judy Garland c) Bette Davis d) Jane Powell e) Debbie Reynolds
ANS: TIE BETWEEN LAKE AND GARLAND, BOTH 4'11 1/2." DAVIS WAS 5'3", POWELL 5'1" AND REYNOLDS 5'2".

17) Nicole Kidman is famous for her 5'11" height. Who is the tallest of the following actresses?
a) Sophia Loren b) Audrey Hepburn c) Geena Davis d) Sandra Bullock e) Catherine Zeta-Jones
ANS: C. GEENA DAVIS TOPS THEM ALL AT 6'0." LOREN IS 5'9," HEPBURN 5'7", BULLOCK 5'7 1/2" AND ZETA-JONES 5'8 1/2".

18) A fan rushed up to an actress and said, "I've heard so much about you." And the actress replied, "Yeah, but you can't prove a thing." Who was the actress?
ANS: MAE WEST.

19) What two glamorous actresses were Frank Sinatra's co-stars in "Pal Joey?"
ANS: RITA HAYWORTH AND KIM NOVAK.

20) What historical character did Bette Davis play in two different films?
ANS: QUEEN ELIZABETH I ("THE PRIVATE LIVES OF ELIZABETH AND ESSEX" IN 1939; "THE VIRGIN QUEEN" IN 1955).

LUISE RAINER

NICOLE KIDMAN

21) Luise Rainer holds a unique distinction in Oscar history. What is it?
ANS: SHE WAS THE FIRST ACTOR TO WIN OSCARS TWO YEARS IN A ROW. ("THE GREAT ZIEGFELD" IN 1936, "THE GOOD EARTH" IN 1937).

22) Cyd Charisse did not dance with Gene Kelly in which of the following movies: a) "Singin' in the Rain" b) "It's Always Fair Weather" c) "Les Girls"
ANS: C

23) Her screen credit in the James Bond movie, "Live and Let Die," was "Introducing..." but she became famous for her TV role as "Dr. Quinn, Medicine Woman."
ANS: JANE SEYMOUR.

24) She was in the James Bond film, "Never Say Never Again" and later won an Academy Award for her role in "L.A. Confidential." Name the actress.
ANS: KIM BASINGER.

25) Kathy Nolan was the female lead in the popular 1950s sitcom, "The Real McCoys." But her claim to fame in the movie business is rather unique. What is it?
ANS: SHE WAS THE FIRST WOMAN EVER ELECTED PRESIDENT OF THE SCREEN ACTORS GUILD. (1975).

KATHY NOLAN

26) While Yvonne Craig was

dating Elvis Presley she appeared in two of his movies, but she gained fame for a television role. What was it?
ANS: BATGIRL IN THE "BATMAN" SERIES.

27) What glamorous actress of the 1940s became a pioneer in the field of wireless communication through her co-invention of spread spectrum technology?
ANS: HEDY LAMARR.

BARBARA STANWYCK

28) She is credited for being the first "Bond Girl."
ANS: URSULA ANDRESS.

29) Another "Bond Girl" learned she had won an Academy Award in 2002 while she was filming the Bond film, "Die Another Day." Who was she?
ANS: HALLE BERRY.

AMY ADAMS

30) Lois Maxwell appeared in 14 James Bond movies as "Miss Moneypenny," M's secretary. Of the following actresses, which also made more than one appearance as "Miss Moneypenny" in a James Bond movie?
a) Caroline Bliss b) Barbara Bouchet c) Pamela Salem d) Shirley Eaton
ANS: A

31) Who was considered for the Judy Garland role in "The

HALLE BERRY

Wizard of Oz?"
a) Shirley Temple b) Bonita Granville c) Virginia Weidler d) Kathryn Grayson
ANS:A

32) The star of the movie, "Mame," was:
a) Rosalind Russell b) Lucille Ball c) Angela Lansbury d) Mary Martin
ANS: B

33) How many times did Ingrid Bergman play Joan of Arc in a film?
a) 2 b) 3 c) 1 d) 0
ANS: A. IN THE 1948 FILM, "JOAN OF ARC" AND IN THE 1954 PRODUCTION, "GIOVANNA D'ARCO AL ROGO."

34) Actress Amy Adams was born in:
a) Italy b) England c) Germany d) China
ANS: VICENZA, ITALY.

35) Her bombastic style prompted Bob Hope to call her "A vitamin pill with legs."
a) Ethel Merman b) Betty Grable c) Betty Hutton d) Martha Raye
ANS: C

URSULA ANDRESS

36) Though she starred in 48 films during a 20 year period, she did not get the role of Eliza in the 1938 film, "Pygmalion," even though its author, George Bernard Shaw,

favored her for the part.
a) Norma Shearer b) Marion Davies c) Mary Astor d) Billie Dove
ANS: B

37) Doris Day's co-star in "The Winning Team" was:
a) Jack Lemmon b) Rock Hudson c) George Brent d) Ronald Reagan
ANS. D

LILLIE LANGTRY

38) What do these three films have in common?
"Storm Warning" – "April in Paris" – "I'll See You in My Dreams"
ANS: DORIS DAY WAS IN ALL OF THEM.

39) Jeanne Eagels was a famous stage beauty around the turn of the last century. Who played her in her life-story 1957 movie?
ANS: KIM NOVAK.

LOLA ALBRIGHT

40) The famous English-Victorian actress, Lillie Langtry, was portrayed in two films. What were they?
ANS: "THE WESTERNER" AND "THE LIFE AND TIMES OF JUDGE ROY BEAN."

41) Did Lillie Langtry ever appear in a film of her own?
ANS: YES, "HIS NEIGHBOR'S WIFE," IN 1913, WHEN SHE WAS 60.

42) Who was the actress who played Sylvia Trench in the

DORIS DAY

James Bond films?
a) Zena Marshall b) Eunice Grayson c) Ursula Andress d) Daniela Bianchi
ANS: B.

43) Of these four leading ladies, which one never appeared in a silent movie:
a) Loretta Young b) Myrna Loy c) Katharine Hepburn d) Barbara Stanwyck
ANS: C

44) One character-actor is credited with appearing in the most Doris Day films. Who is he?
a) Franklin Pangborn b) Edward Everett Horton c) S. Z. Sakall d) Leon Ames
ANS: C (4 FILMS).

45) True or False: Lola Albright was a singing extra at MGM long before she portrayed the sultry nightclub singer Edie Hart in the TV series, "Peter Gunn."
ANS: TRUE. LOLA RELEASED TWO ALBUMS WHILE CO-STARRING IN THE SERIES.

46) Who were the leading ladies in Herbert Lom, Claude Rains, Lon Chaney Sr. and Gerard Butler's "Phantom of the Opera" films?
ANS: LOM (HEATHER SEARS); RAINS (SUSANNA FOSTER); CHANEY (MARY PHILBIN); BUTLER (EMMY ROSSUM).

MAE WEST

47) Who played John Barry-
more, Fredric March and
Spencer Tracy's leading ladies
in their "Dr. Jekyll and Mr.
Hyde" films?
ANS: BARRYMORE (NITA NALDI);
MARCH (MIRIAM HOPKINS); TRACY
(INGRID BERGMAN).

48) During the early 1960s,
what actress was the leading
box office star four times, from
1960 through 1965?
a) Katharine Hepburn
b) Grace Kelly c) Doris Day
d) Audrey Hepburn
ANS: C

TINA LOUISE

49) How many films did Mae West make with Cary
Grant?
a) 1 b) 3 c) 2 d) None
ANS: C, "SHE DONE HIM WRONG" AND "I'M NO ANGEL," BOTH
IN 1933.

50) Who did Doris Day replace
for the lead role in "Romance
on the High Seas?"
a) Judy Garland b) Betty Hutton c) Joan Blondell d) Marilyn Maxwell
ANS: B

51) Tina Louise had many
screen credits, including
"God's Little Acre," before she
became a popular regular in
what television series?
ANS: "GILLIGAN'S ISLAND."

LORETTA YOUNG

52) All but one of the following leading men made more than one film with Doris Day.
a) Gordon MacRae b) Jack Carson c) James Cagney d) Jack Lemmon
ANS: D

53) What actress made the most movies with Cary Grant?
a) Loretta Young b) Ingrid Bergman c) Katharine Hepburn d) Deborah Kerr
ANS: C (4 FILMS).

54) Ida Lupino gained fame as an actress early in her career, but later she added another credit to her portfolio. What was it?
ANS: AS A DIRECTOR OF SEVEN FEATURE FILMS.

55) Who played Fanny Brice in the biography of that comedienne?
ANS) BARBRA STREISAND IN "FUNNY GIRL."

56) Kirsten Dunst played Marie Antoinette in the 2006 film of that name. Who played the ill-fated

EMMA THOMPSON

NATALIE PORTMAN

French queen in the 1938 version?
ANS: NORMA SHEARER.

57) What historical figure did Greer Garson play in "Sunrise at Campobello?"
ANS: ELEANOR ROOSEVELT.

58) Who played Billy Holiday in her bio, the 1972 film, "Lady Sings the Blues?"
ANS: DIANA ROSS.

59) Who played the title role in "The Song of Bernadette?"
ANS: JENNIFER JONES.

JANE RUSSELL

60) In real life, Elsa Lancaster was married to Charles Laughton. In what film was she married to Boris Karloff?
ANS: "BRIDE OF FRANKENSTEIN."

61) Which two of these actresses played Cleopatra in films of that name?
a) Elizabeth Taylor and Hedy Lamarr b) Elizabeth Taylor and Claudette Colbert c) Elizabeth Taylor and Myrna Loy d) Linda Darnell and Joan Crawford
ANS: B

62) Marlene Dietrich's breakthrough film, "Blue Angel," was made in what country?
a) England b) Austria c) Germany d) USA

HILLARY SWANK

ANS: C

63) Who played the title role of Amelia Earhart in the 2009 film, "Amelia?"
ANS: HILARY SWANK.

64) Brian Aherne played Emperor Maximilian in the film, "Juarez." Who played his wife, Empress Carlotta?
ANS: BETTE DAVIS.

65) She played musical star Lillian Russell in the 1940 film of that name.
ANS: ALICE FAYE.

DIANA ROSS

66) Morgan Brittany portrayed what famous English actress in back to back films in 1975 and 1976?
ANS: VIVIEN LEIGH.

RENE ZELLWEGER

67) She was the highest grossing actor of 2014, with her movies having grossed more than $1.4-billion world-wide.
ANS: JENNIFER LAWRENCE.

68) Who was the Italian actress who played the fiancé of Orson Welles in "The Third Man?"
a) Ann Magnani b) Sophia Loren c) Claudia Cardinale d) Alida Valli
ANS: D

69) Emma Thompson appeared in four films directed by her then husband: "Henry V," (1989), "Dead Again," (1994), "Peter's Friends," (1992) and "Much Ado About Nothing," (1993). Who was he?

ANS: KENNETH BRANAGH.

70) Renee Zellweger, John C. Riley and Catherine Zeta-Jones all were nominated for Oscars for "Chicago" in 2002. Did any of them win an award?

ANS: YES, ZETA-JONES WON BEST SUPPORTING ACTRESS.

71) Barbara Stanwyck and Betty Hutton played what iconic western character in different movies?

ANS: ANNIE OAKLEY.

72) Who said it: "Acting is the most minor of gifts. After all, Shirley Temple could do it when she was four."
a) Katharine Hepburn b) Bette Davis c) Barbara Stanwyck d) Ethel Barrymore

ANS: A

ELIZABETH TAYLOR   AVA GARDNER

JUDY DENCH

73) How old was Elizabeth Taylor when she made her first film?
a) 18 b) 10 c) 12 d)15
ANS: B

74) Judy Garland appeared in her first movie in what year?
a) 1935 b) 1940 c) 1929 d) 1930
ANS: C

75) Her first two film roles were the female leads in "Oklahoma" and "Carousel." Who was the actress?
ANS: SHIRLEY JONES.

76) What actress played the title role in "All About Eve?"
ANS: ANNE BAXTER.

77) Helen Mirren and Maggie Smith were nominated for Best Supporting Actress in 2001 in the same movie. What was it?
ANS: "GOSFORD PARK."

78) Who played the female lead in "Citizen Kane?"
ANS: DOROTHY COMINGORE.

79) How many Oscar nominations did Tallulah Bankhead get?
ANS: NONE.

80) Who did Meryl Streep replace for the lead role in the

JOANNE WOODWARD

1999 film, "Music of the Heart?"
a) Cher b) Madonna c) Julia Roberts d) Debra Winger
ANS: B

81) Who was the female lead in "Butch Cassidy and the Sundance Kid?"
ANS: KATHARINE ROSS.

82) In which of the following films did Faye Dunaway not appear?
a) "Chinatown" b) "Willow" c) "Supergirl" d) "Don Juan DeMarco"
ANS: B

KIM BASSINGER

83) Imdb.com lists her at 50th in its list of the 50 greatest actresses, but says "She probably was the most celebrated of all actresses. Who is she?
a) Hedy Lamarr b) Betty Grable c) Marilyn Monroe d) Deborah Kerr
ANS: C

84) In what film did Kate Winslet and Judy Dench play the same character?
ANS: "IRIS" IN 2001.

85) She was Hugh Grant's love interest in "Sense and Sensibility," 1995, and his sister in "Love Actually," 2003.
ANS: EMMA THOMPSON.

KIM NOVAK

BETTY GRABLE   MARILYN MONROE

86) How many of the Godfather films did Diane Keaton appear in?
ANS: ALL THREE.

87) She has worked with nine directors who have won Best Director Oscars.
a) Bette Davis b) Meryl Streep c) Cate Blanchett d) Julianne Moore
ANS: C

88) Natalie Portman was born in:
a) London b) Cairo c) Jerusalem d) New York City
ANS: C

89) Has Shirley MacLaine ever made a movie with her brother, Warren Beatty?
ANS: NO.

90) Jane Wyman, who was a registered Republican, says that her marriage broke up to what actor, because he was a registered Democrat at the time?
ANS: RONALD REAGAN.

DEBBIE REYNOLDS

91) Nicole Kidman is Australian, but she wasn't born in that country. Where was she born?
a) London b) Honolulu c) Bejing d) Tokyo
ANS: B

92) Who is the female member of the Huston acting-directing that includes Walter and John?
ANS: ANJELICA.

93) What actress was Charles Boyer "gaslighting" in "Gaslight?"
a) Angela Lansbury b) Marlene Dietrich c) Ingrid Bergman d) Mary Astor
ANS: C

94) Irene Dunne and Kathryn Grayson played Magnolia in different versions of what film?
ANS: "SHOW BOAT."

95) Who are Jamie Lee Curtis' mother and father?
ANS: JANET LEIGH AND TONY CURTIS.

96) How old was Debbie Reynolds when she co-starred in "Singin' in the Rain?"
a) 22 b) 16 c) 25 d) 19
ANS: D

97) What actress insured her legs for a million dollars?

GRACE KELLY

a) Marilyn Monroe b) Marlene Dietrich c) Betty Grable d) Leslie Caron
ANS: C

98) What actress played "Pvt. Benjamin?"
ANS: GOLDIE HAWN.

99) Sarah Jessica Parker says her favorite Hitchcock film is:
a) "North by Northwest"
b) "Notorious" c) "Rebecca"
d) "Rear Window"
ANS: C

PATRICIA ARQUETTE

100) Who said, "I've often been mistaken for Meryl Streep, although never on Oscar night?"
ANS: GLENN CLOSE.

101) Janet Leigh was discovered by what actress?
a) Miriam Hopkins b) Joan Crawford c) Norma Shearer d) Loretta Young
ANS: C

102) The best paid actress of the 1990s was:
a) Sandra Bullock b) Julia Roberts c) Demi Moore
d) Meryl Streep
ANS: B

103) She was born in downtown Los Angeles and was a third-generation American, but she is considered the first Chinese movie star. What was

MARY MARTIN

her name?
ANS: ANNA MAY WONG.

104) Geraldine Chaplin, Charlie's fourth child, played Hannah Chaplin in the 1992 film biography, "Chaplin." Who was Hannah?
a) Her mother b) Her aunt c) Her grandmother
d) A fictitious character
ANS: C

105) She was known as the "Queen of Scream," probably for her role in the 1933 film that saved RKO from bankruptcy.
a) Fay Wray b) Elsa Lancaster c) Simone Simone
d) Dolores del Rio
ANS: A ("KING KONG" WAS THE FILM.)

106) Famed movie mogul Daryl F. Zanuck called her "Unquestionably, the most beautiful woman in movie history."
a) Ava Gardner b) Hedy Lamarr c) Elizabeth Taylor
d) Gene Tierney
ANS: D

GENE TIERNEY   HEDY LAMARR

ANNA MAY WONG

107) Although she was born in India, her most famous film role was that of a Southern belle during the Civil War.
a) Olivia De Havilland
b) Vivien Leigh c) Miriam Hopkins d) Norma Shearer
ANS: B

108) True or False: Patricia Arquette is the granddaughter of TV character "Charley Weaver," whose real name was Cliff Arquette.
ANS: TRUE.

109) Her movies were banned in Monaco by order of the country's ruler, Prince Rainier.
a) Jane Russell b) Meryl Streep c) Grace Kelly
d) Marilyn Monroe
ANS: C

110) She was born in Sweden, discovered by actor-comedian George Burns in Chicago and uses only her first name.
a) Cher b) Ann-Margaret
c) Beyonce d) Madonna
ANS: B

111) Who said it about her sister: "With all of Constance's juggling of dates over the years, I started out as the youngest, then became her twin and finally wound up as the oldest sister."

EVA MARIE SAINT

ANS: JOAN BENNETT.

112) Nicole Kidman reportedly said after her divorce from what actor, "Now I can wear high heels again."
ANS: TOM CRUISE.

113) She became the first actress to appear on the cover of Life Magazine, the May of 1937 issue.
a) Bette Davis b) Jean Harlow c) Joan Crawford d) Betty Grable
ANS: B

JOAN CRAWFORD

114) She was in the Ziegfeld Follies at age 13, was one of the original 20 Goldwyn Girls, was considered for the Scarlett O'Hara role in "Gone With the Wind," had an extensive film career and was married for six years to Charlie Chaplin.
a) Lucille Ball b) Betty Grable c) Ann Dvorak d) Paulette Goddard
ANS: D

115) Alfred Hitchcock's preference for blonde leading ladies is well known. In "Psycho" he featured two of them. One was Janet Leigh. Who was the other?
ANS: VERA MILES.

116) Although she had a long and varied career in both films and television, she will probably always be remembered for her first movie, "The Outlaw."
ANS: JANE RUSSELL.

JANET LEIGH

VERA MILES

117) Two actresses are tied for appearing in the most films directed by Alfred Hitchcock. Can you name them?
a) Tippi Hedren and Ingrid Bergman b) Grace Kelly and Joan Fontaine c) Ingrid Bergman and Grace Kelly d) Eva Marie Saint and Priscilla Lane
ANS: C

118) Doris Day's first dramatic appearance was in the 1950 film, "Young Man with a Horn." Who played the young man?
a) Gordon MacRae b) Jack Lemmon c) Jack Carson d) Kirk Douglas
ANS: D

IRENE DUNNE

119) She was named "The Most Beautiful Face of 2007" but she had already portrayed a film beauty in 2004 when

JULIA ROBERTS

she played Ava Gardner in "The Aviator." Name her.
a) Megan Fox b) Kate Mara
c) Kate Beckinsale d) Penelope Cruz
ANS: C

120) Eva Marie Saint said this about which one of her co-stars: "Adorable! A dear man and funny. Probably the most elegant man I've ever worked with — or even met."
a) Richard Burton b) James Garner c) Gregory Peck
d) Cary Grant
ANS: D

121) She had an operatic singing voice but seldom got the chance to use it in a movie save for some of her early films, inclcluding the role of Magnolia in the 1936 version of "Show Boat." Who was she?
ANS: IRENE DUNNE.

KATE WINSLET

SHIRLEY JONES

FAY WRAY   ANN-MARGARET

122) Shirley Jones' portrayal of Lulu Bains was a complete change of pace from the musicals and light comedies she had been in. What was the film in which she played Lulu?
ANS: "ELMER GANTRY."

123) Judy Garland was a first cousin, three times removed, of a famous U. S. president. Can you

name him?
a) John F. Kennedy b) Dwight D. Eisenhower c) U. S. Grant d) Woodrow Wilson
ANS: C

124) This French actress was called "The princess of pout" by Time Magazine.
a) Juliette Binoche b) Jeanne Moreau c) Brigitte Bardot d) Isabelle Adjani
ANS: C

JUDY GARLAND

125) She played the title role in the eight Mexican spitfire films that were made from 1939 to 1943. Name her.
a) Rita Hayworth b) Dolores del Rio c) Lupe Velez d) Ida Lupino
ANS: C

126) Band leader and clarinetist Artie Shaw had several wives, all of whom were glamorous actresses. Which one of these was not one of them?
a) Ava Gardner b) Evelyn Keyes c) Gene Tierney d) Lana Turner
ANS: C

SANDRA BULLOCK

127) Helen Hayes was known as "The First Lady of the Theater." Who was known as "The First Lady of the Screen?"
a) Bette Davis b) Loretta Young c) Norma Shearer d) Joan Crawford
ANS: C

NORMA SHEARER

128) "Becky Sharp," released in 1935, is considered to be the first full Technicolor film. Who played the title role?
a) Bette Davis b) Carol Lombard c) Miriam Hopkins d) Ann Sheridan
ANS: C

129) One of the following actresses did not get her career start in a small role in an

Andy Hardy movie.
a) Lana Turner b) Kathryn
Grayson c) Judy Garland
d) Esther Williams
ANS: C

130) Jean Arthur, Frances
Farmer, Yvonne DeCarlo,
Evelyn Ankers and Jane Russell have all played the same
historical character. Who was
she?
ANS: CALAMITY JANE.

131) "The Sarong Girl" was
the nickname for what ac-
tress?
a) Linda Darnell b) Cyd Charisse c) Dorothy Lamour d) Jeanne Crain
ANS: C

MIRIAM HOPKINS

132) She portrayed the title character in the 1935
version of "She" and later became a Congress-
woman from California who lost the 1950 election
for the U.S. Senate to Richard Nixon.
ANS: HELEN GAHAGAN (DOUGLAS).

133) Of the three Talmadge sisters, Norma, Con-
stance and Natalie, Norma, in 1927, tripped in
some fresh-laid cement and started a tradition.
What was it?
ANS: HAND AND FOOTPRINTS IN FRONT OF GRAUMAN'S CHI-
NESE THEATER.

134) Sandra Bullock became one of 17 actors who
have won an Oscar for portraying a living person.
What was the name of the film she was in?
ANS: "THE BLIND SIDE."

Co-Stars

1) Cary Grant and Sophia Loren co-starred with what actor in "The Pride and the Passion"?
ANS: FRANK SINATRA.

2) Russell Crowe and Denzel Washington appeared in what films together?
ANS: "VIRTUOSITY" AND "AMERICAN GANGSTER."

SOPHIA LOREN

3) Which one of these actors has not (as yet) co-starred with Meg Ryan?
a) Tom Hanks b) George Clooney c) Nicolas Cage
d) Andy Garcia
ANS: B

4) Which one of her following co-stars appeared in more than one film with Doris Day?
a) Brian Keith b) Gordon MacRae c) Cary Grant
d) James Stewart
ANS: B

5) What real-life character did Leonardo Di Caprio and Jason Robards both portray in films?
ANS: HOWARD HUGHES.

6) With which of the following actors has Charlize Theron not co-starred?
a) Al Pacino b) Woody Allen c) Bill Paxton
d) Orlando Bloom
ANS: D

7) Who played Knute Rockne in the film in which Ronald Reagan played "The Gipper?"
ANS: PAT O'BRIEN.

8) Cary Grant made separate movies with which one of these sister-teams?
a) Olivia De Havilland and Joan Fontaine b) The Andrews Sisters c) Constance and Joan Bennett
ANS: C

9) Deborah Kerr and Yul Brynner co-starred in "The King and I." Who played their roles in "Anna

FRED ASTAIRE AND GINGER ROGERS

DEBORAH KERR

and the King of Siam?"
ANS: IRENE DUNNE AND REX
HARRISON.

10) Which of these actors did
not co-star in a film with
Grace Kelly?
a) Cary Grant b) Gary Cooper
c) Bing Crosby d) Robert Taylor
ANS: D

11) Who was Marilyn Monroe's
co-star in "Bus Stop?"
a) Don Murray b) Jack Lemmon c) David Wayne d) Tom Ewell
ANS: A

12) Reese Witherspoon made two English period
films, "The Importance of Being Earnest" and "Van-
ity Fair." Who was her co-star in the latter?
a) Jeremy Irons b) Colin Firth c) Gabriel Byrne
d) Rupert Everett
ANS: C

13) In what movie did the two
Kevins – Kline and Costner –
co-star?
ANS: "SILVERADO."

14) What actor co-starred in
films with the two Hepburns,
Katharine and Audrey?
a) Clark Gable b) Gary Cooper
c) Cary Grant d) Robert
Mitchum
ANS: C

YUL BRYNNER

15) Who co-starred in the most films together?
a) Spencer Tracy and Katharine Hepburn b) Myrna Loy and William Powell c) Penny Singleton and Arthur Lake
ANS: C (28)

16) What actor co-starred in the most films with Doris Day?
a) Gordon MacRae b) Rock Hudson c) James Cagney d) Tony Randall
ANS: A. GORDON MAC RAE (5).

17) Which of the following actresses co-starred with Cary Grant in more than one film?
a) Marlene Dietrich b) Grace Kelly c) Ingrid Bergman d) Doris Day
ANS: C

18) Who was Cher's romantic interest in "Moonstruck?"
ANS: NICHOLAS CAGE.

19) Who co-starred with Mario Lanza in his first

PAUL HENREID, INGRID BERGMAN AND
HUMPHREY BOGART IN "CASABLANCA"

ELIZABETH TAYLOR AND SPENCER TRACY IN "FATHER OF THE BRIDE," 1950.

two films?
a) Judy Garland
b) Ava Gardner
c) Kathryn Grayson
d) Jane Powell
ANS: C

20) Jeanette Mac-Donald and Nelson Eddy co-starred in eight films. What was the first one?
a) "Rose-Marie"
b) "Maytime"
c) "Naughty Marietta" d) "New Moon"
ANS: C

21) How many films did Sophia Loren and Marcello Mastroianni make together?
a) 10 b) 15) c)12 d) 17
ANS: D

22) Fred Astaire and Gene Kelly appeared in two films together. Can you name them?
ANS: "ZIEGFELD :FOLLIES" IN 1946 AND "THAT'S ENTERTINMENT II" IN 1976.

23) Barbara Stanwyck and Fred MacMurray made "Double Indemnity" in 1944. They co-starred in two other films. What were they?
a) "Meet John Doe" and "Ball of Fire" b) "There's Always Tomor-

FRED MAC MURRAY

HUMPHREY BOGART AND LAUREN BACALL IN
"TO HAVE AND HAVE NOT"

row" and "Remember the Night" c) "The Lady Eve"
and "Suddenly It's Spring" d) "Practically Yours"
and "Breakfast for Two"
ANS: B

24) What was the last film Humphrey Bogart and
Lauren Bacall made together?
ANS: "KEY LARGO" IN 1942.

25) Who co-starred as Dr.
Gillespie with Lew Ayres in
the Dr. Kildare series of
movies?
ANS: LIONEL BARRYMORE.

26) She co-starred with her
then-husband, Tony Curtis, in
five films, "Houdini" (1953),
"The Black Shield of Fal-
worth" (1954), "The Vikings"
(1958), "The Perfect
Furlough" (1958), and "Who

CLAIRE TREVOR

GRETA GARBO AND
JOHN GILBERT IN
"A WOMAN OF
AFFAIRS"

Was That Lady?" (1960). They also had cameos together in a sixth film, "Pepe" (1960). Who was she?
ANS: JANET LEIGH.

27) Which of these actors and actresses actually made a film together?
a) Cher and Frank Sinatra b) Barbra Streisand and Tony Bennett c) Madonna and Sean Penn d) Lady Gaga and Ben Affleck
ANS: C. THEY CO-STARRED IN "SHANGHAI SURPRISE" IN 1986.

28) Johhny Weissmuller played Tarzan in 12 films. Who co-starred with him as Jane in the first six of those 12?
a) Maureen O'Hara b) Maureen O'Sullivan c) Fay Wray d) Linda Darnell
ANS: B

CLARK GABLE AND
VIVIEN LEIGH IN
"GONE WITH
THE WIND"

29) How many films did Judy Garland and Mickey Rooney make together?
a) 5 b) 12 c) 9 d) 7
ANS: C

30) What was the only film to co-star W. C. Fields and Mae West?
ANS: "MY LITTLE CHICKADEE" IN 1940.

31) What was the first movie that Elizabeth Taylor co-

starred with Richard Burton?
ANS: "CLEOPATRA" IN 1963.

32) They made 11 films together and Bette Davis is said
to have regarded him as her
favorite leading man.
a) James Cagney b) Paul Henreid c) George Brent d) Herbert Marshall
ANS: C

W. C. FIELDS

33) Claire Trevor had a memo-
rable role opposite Edward G.
Robinson in the 1948 film,
"Key Largo." In how many
other films did they co-star?
a) 4 b) 2 c) 1 d) None
ANS: B

34) Who was Deanna Durbin's co-star in three of
her films?
a) Robert Cummings b) Joel McCrea c) Mickey
Rooney d) Fred MacMurray
ANS: A

35) Dennis Morgan and Jack
Carson teamed up in 11 films.
Who was their female co-star
in four of them?
a) Virginia Mayo b) Ida
Lupino c) Priscilla Lane d)
Ann Sheridan
ANS: D

36) Errol Flynn and Olivia De
Havilland made nine movies
together. What was the first

JEAN HARLOW

MAUREEN O'HARA

one?
a) "They Died With Their Boots On" b) "That Forsythe Woman" c) "Captain Blood" d) "The Adventures of Robin Hood"
ANS: C, IN 1935.

37) Although they weren't a true team in their first film together, "The Secret Six" in 1931, how many films did Clark Gable and Jean Harlow make together?
a) 3 b) 6 c) 5 d) 8

ANS: B

38) They co-starred in six films but it was almost 50 years between the first and last time Maureen O'Hara and Anthony Quinn appeared together. What was their last film together?
a) "The Black Swan" b) "Against All Flags" c) "Sinbad the Sailor" d) "Only the Lonely"
ANS: D

39) Of Charles Boyer and Ingrid Bergman's three films together, was "Arch of Triumph" (1948) their first, second or third co-starring film?
ANS: THEIR SECOND. "GASLIGHT" WAS FIRST, "A MATTER OF TIME," THIRD.

40) Victor McLaglen and Edmund Lowe made 13 films together, starting with the silent 1926 feature, "What Price Glory." Their final film together

LANA TURNER

RICHARD BURTON

was in 1956. What was it?
a) "How the West Was Won" b) "Around the World in 80 Days" c) "Prince Valiant" d) "She Wore a Yellow Ribbon"
ANS: B

41) Clark Gable and Lana Turner co-starred in four films, but only one was in Technicolor. Which one was it? a) "Betrayed" b) "Somewhere I'll Find You" c) "Homecoming" d) "Honky Tonk"
ANS: A

42) Which of the four Lane sisters — Leota, Lola, Rosemary and Priscilla — co-starred in four films?
ANS: LOLA, ROSEMARY AND PRISCILLA.

43) Which of the following did not co-star in a film? a) George Clooney and Rene Zelwegger b) Roger Moore and Judy Dench c) Cary Grant and Shirley Temple
ANS: B

ELIZABETH TAYLOR AND ROBERT TAYLOR IN "IVANHOE"

44) What did the stars of the 1952 film, "Ivanhoe," have in common?
ANS: ROBERT TAYLOR AND ELIZA-BETH TAYLOR SHARED THE SAME LAST NAME.

45) Meg Ryan starred with Tom Hanks in "Sleepless in Seattle" and "You've Got Mail." Name another film in which they co-starred.
ANS: "JOE VS. THE VOLCANO."

MARLON BRANDO

46) They co-starred in four films, including "Reap the Wild Wind" in 1942, and "Kitty" in 1945.
a) Marlene Dietrich and James Stewart b) Ava Gardner and Clark Gable c) Paulette Goddard and Ray Milland d) Joan Crawford and Gary Cooper
ANS: C

47) Walter Pidgeon played the husband of what actress in seven of the eight films they made together?
a) Green Garson b) Myrna Loy c) Deborah Kerr d) Joan Bennett
ANS: A

48) Although they were originally scheduled to have their singing voices dubbed, she and Marlon Brando did their own singing in "Guys and Dolls." Who was she?
ANS: JEAN SIMMONS.

EMMA STONE

49) Joel McCrea co-starred with

this actress six times.
Who was she?
a) Miriam Hopkins
b) Constance Bennett
c) Claudette Colbert
d) Barbara Stanwyck
ANS: D

WILLIAM POWELL AND
MYRNA LOY IN
"THE THIN MAN"

50) What leading man co-starred with Greta Garbo the most times?
a) John Gilbert b) John Barrymore c) Robert Taylor d) Melvyn Douglas
ANS: A. FOUR TIMES.

51) True or False: Helena Bonham Carter and Johnny Depp have appeared in four movies together.
ANS: TRUE.

52) How many films besides "Godfather II" did Al Pacino and Robert De Niro co-star in?

JEAN SIMMONS

a) 4 b) 2 c) 1 d) 0
ANS: B

53) Emma Stone and Ryan Gosling made their third picture together in 2016. What was it?
ANS: "LA LA LAND."

54) Which of the following movies did Frank Sinatra and Gene Kelly not co-star in?
a) "On the Town" b) "Words and Music" c) "Take Me Out to the Ball Game" d) "Anchors

PRISCILLA LANE

Away"
ANS: B

55) Esther Williams and Van Johnson made how many films together after the first film in which they both appeared, "A Guy Named Joe," in 1943?
a) 3 b) 6 c) 4 d) 2
ANS: C

56) Who did Kathryn Grayson co-star with in the 1942 film, "Rio Rita?"
a) Howard Keel b) Mario Lanza c) The Marx Brothers d) Abbott and Costello
ANS: D

57) Spencer Tracy and Elizabeth Taylor co-starred as father-daughter in how many films?
a) 1 b) 2) c) 3 d) None
ANS: B

CARY GRANT, ROSALIND RUSSELL AND RALPH BELLAMY IN "HIS GIRL FRIDAY."

Directors

1) The line, "Ready when you are, C. B.," refers to what director?
ANS: CECIL B. DEMILLE.

2) Director Stanley Kubrick started out as what?
ANS: A STILL PHOTOGRAPHER.

3) This director made "The Miracle Worker" and "Bonnie and Clyde" among many others. Who was he?
ANS: ARTHUR PENN.

ALFRED HITCHCOCK

4) Who was the featured female vocalist in Vincente Minelli's first feature film, the all-black 1943 musical, "Cabin in the Sky?"
a) Lena Horne b) Billy Holiday
c) Dorothy Dandridge
d) Hattie McDaniel
ANS: A

5) Blake Edwards' "The Pink

Panther" series was a milestone in movie comedies. Name a drama he directed that starred Jack Lemmon.
ANS: "THE DAYS OF WINE AND ROSES."

6) What popular movie did Robert Altman direct that later became a hit TV series?
ANS: "MASH."

7) From what university did Frank Capra get an engineering degree?
a) MIT b) Georgia Tech
c) Caltech d) Carnegie Tech
ANS: C

LENA HORNE

8) What director was famous for "storyboarding" his shots before he started filming?
ANS: ALFRED HITCHCOCK.

9) Who directed "Casablanca?"
ANS: MICHAEL CURTIZ.

10) Ron Howard won an Oscar for directing what film?
ANS: "A BEAUTIFUL MIND."

11) What do these personalities have in common in addition to all being directors: Woody Allen, Albert Brooks and Erich von Stroheim.
ANS: THEY ALL APPEARED IN THEIR OWN FILMS.

12) What film was Danny De Vito's directorial debut?

CECIL B. DE MILLE

a) "Throw Momma From the Train" b) "Head Office" c) "Tin Men" d) "Twins"
ANS: A

13) Directors Ridley Scott and Tony Scott are:
a) Not related b) Brothers
c) Cousins d) Father and Son
ANS: B

14) Apparently director Martin Scorsese likes "The" in his titles. But which one of the following did he not direct?
a) "The Last Waltz" b) "The Age of Innocence"
c) "The Hand"
ANS: B

WOODY ALLEN

15) The first American woman to be nominated for a Best Director Academy Award was:
a) Sofia Coppola b) Martha Coolidge c) Randa Haines d) Kathryn Bigelow
ANS: A

BILLY WILDER

16) Actor Charles Laughton directed only one film during his career. It was:
a) "Les Miserables" b) "Night of the Hunter" c) "Rembrandt" d) "Ruggles of Red Gap"
ANS: B

17) British director Frank Oz did voices for the Muppets and what other films?
a) "The Dark Crystal" b) "Star Wars" c) "Bowfinger"

ANS: B

CHARLES LAUGHTON

18) Of only four women to be nominated for a Best Director Oscar, who is the first (and only up to 2016) woman to win the award?
ANS: KATHRYN BIGELOW IN 2007 FOR "THE HURT LOCKER."

19) How old was John Singleton when he was nominated for a Director's Oscar?
a) 26 b) 24 c) 30 d) 28
ANS: B

20) What is the common thread in these three films directed by Charles Vidor: "Cover Girl," "Gilda" and "The Loves of Carmen"
ANS: ALL STARRED RITA HAYWORTH.

21) What director said, in picking up the phone, "I'm out but call me back in an hour."
a) Samuel Goldwyn b) Ernst Lubitsch c) Otto Preminger d) Michael Curtiz
ANS: D

22) How many films has Woody Allen directed, through 2016?
a) 35 b) 52 c) 47 d) 38
ANS: C

23) Who directed "Pretty Woman?"
ANS: GARRY MARSHALL.

GENE KELLY

24) Billy Wilder was a native of what country?
a) England b) USA c) Austria d) Germany
ANS: C

25) He was primarily known as a dancer-actor, but he had several directorial credits. Who was he?
a) Fred Astaire b) Gene Kelly c) Dan Dailey d) George Murphy
ANS: B

STEVEN SPIELBERG

26) It was the only film directed by stage director George S. Kaufman and starred William Powell in 1947.
ANS: "THE SENATOR WAS INDISCREET."

27) Who did writer-director-producer Billy Wilder say was the greatest actor who ever lived?
a) Marlon Brando b) Laurence Olivier c) Charles Laughton d) Jack Lemmon
ANS: C

28) What director made it a point to do a brief cameo in each of his films?
ANS: ALFRED HITCHCOCK.

29) Who directed "Laura?"
ANS: OTTO PREMINGER.

30) Who was the replacement director for both "The Wizard of Oz" and "Gone With the

JOAN FONTAINE

KATHRYN BIGELOW

Wind?"
a) King Vidor b) John Ford
c) Victor Fleming d) William Wyler
ANS: C

31) What film was Robert Redford's directorial debut?
a) "A River Runs Through It"
b) "Ordinary People" c) "Quiz Show"
ANS: B

32) Mihaly Kertesz had directed 64 films in Europe before he was invited to work in America by Warner Bros., where he Anglicized his name to:
ANS: MICHAEL CURTIZ.

33) To what relative did director John Ford start out as an assistant at the beginning of his career?
a) His father b) His uncle c) His brother d) His cousin
ANS: C

34) What was the name of the first feature-length film directed by Steven Spielberg, a movie made for television?
ANS: "DUEL."

35) Alfred Hitchcock liked to star blonde actresses in his films. Which one of these did not appear in one of his movies?
a) Madeline Carroll b) Joan

IDA LUPINO

MICHAEL CURTIZ

Fontaine c) Vera Miles d) Joan Caulfield
ANS: D

36) This director directed a total of 14 different actors in performances which garnered Oscar nominations. Who was he?
a) John Ford b) Billy Wilder c) Steven Spielberg d) Cecil B. DeMille
ANS: B

37) Who did Alfred Hitchcock say was the best director of all times?
a) Steven Spielberg b) Otto Preminger c) John Ford d) Luis Bunuel
ANS: D

38) True or False: Although the Oscars were first given in 1929, no woman had been nominated as Best Director until Italian director Lina Wertmuller was nominated for "Pasqualino Sette Bellezze" ("Seven Beauties") in 1977.
ANS: TRUE. BUT SHE DIDN'T WIN THE AWARD.

39) What actress has appeared in the most films directed by Woody Allen?
ANS: DIANE KEATON HAS APPEARED IN EIGHT, THROUGH 2016.

FRANCIS FORD COPPOLA

40) Who is the first woman to

BUSBY BERKELEY

become a member of the Director's Guild of America?
a) Lina Wertmuller b) Dorothy Arzner c) Ida Lupino
d) Norma Talmadge
ANS: B (1938).

41) Roger Corman set the record for the shortest shooting schedule of a feature film with "The Little Shop of Horrors" in 1960. How many days did it take to shoot?
a) 5 b) 12 c) 8 d) 2
ANS: D

42) What future director was President Woodrow Wilson's personal cinematograper at the Versailles Peace Conference?
a) Cecil B. DeMille b) John Ford c) Victor Fleming
d) Frank Capra
ANS: C

43) Billy Wilder directed seven movies with this actor. Who was he?
a) Jack Lemmon b) Fred MacMurray c) Walter Matthau
d) Spencer Tracy
ANS: A

WALTER MATTHAU

44) Gene Kelly not only acted in "Singin in the Rain," but co-directed the film. With whom?
ANS: STANLEY DONEN.

45) What is the name of the only film directed by Marlon

Brando?
ANS: "ONE-EYED JACKS" IN 1961.

46) Who was the director whose musicals featured intricate kaleidoscopic designs by his dancers?
ANS: BUSBY BERKELEY.

47) Like Chaplin, he was one of the comedy stars of the silent film era. Also like Chaplin, he was a film director. Who was he?
ANS) BUSTER KEATON.

OTTO PREMINGER

48) This director, along with Lee Strasberg, in 1947 started the famous Actor's Studio in New York. Who was he?
a) Preston Sturges b) King Vidor c) Elia Kazan
d) William Wyler
ANS: C

VICTOR FLEMING

49) This director appeared in two Best Picture Oscar winners as an actor.
a) Alfred Hitchcock b) Roger Corman c) Stanley Kubrick
d) John Huston
ANS: B

50) Who directed "The Bridge on the River Kwai" and "Lawrence of Arabia?"
ANS: DAVID LEAN.

51) Who directed the film for which Walter Matthau was

nominated for an acting Oscar?
ANS: JACK LEMMON. THE FILM WAS "KOTCH," 1971.

52) What was Alfred Hitchcock's last movie?
ANS: "FAMILY PLOT."

53) Leo McCarey directed a remake of his 1939 film, "Love Affair," with what new title?
ANS: "AN AFFAIR TO REMEMBER" IN 1957.

ROBERT REDFORD

54) He's almost as famous for his wine making as he is for his film directing. Who is he?
ANS: FRANCIS FORD COPPOLA.

55) He directed her on television and she directed him in movies. They both have directed highly successful motion pictures. They are brother and sister. Name them.
ANS: GARRY AND PENNY MARSHALL.

RITA HAYWORTH

56) He has an impressive list of films he directed, including "It Happened One Night," "Meet John Doe" and "Lost Horizon." But it was a 1946 film, "It's a Wonderful Life," for which he probably will be most remembered. Who is he?
ANS: FRANK CAPRA.

57) From TV actor to Spaghetti western movie star, he turned his talents to directing. Who is he?
ANS: CLINT EASTWOOD.

Great Lines From Great Movies

1) Which one of the following lines was not spoken by Humphrey Bogart in a film?
a) "Here's looking at you kid." b) "The stuff that dreams are made of." c) "Round up the usual suspects."
ANS: C

2) In what movie did Greta Garbo say, "I want to be alone?"
ANS: "GRAND HOTEL."

3) Who said, "I am big! It's the pictures that got small!"
ANS: GLORIA SWANSON AS NORMA DESMOND IN "SUNSET BOULE-VARD."

4) Orson Welles' famous one word line as "Citizen Kane"

GRETA GARBO

SIDNEY POITIER

was?
ANS: "ROSEBUD."

5) What was the movie in which the line was "Show me the money?"
ANS: "JERRY MAGUIRE."

6) What actress said, "After all, tomorrow is another day."
a) Vivien Leigh b) Bette Davis c) Lauren Bacall d) Joan Crawford
ANS: A

7) Was it Robert DeNiro or Marlon Brando, as Don Vito Corleone, who first said. "I'm going to make him an offer he can't refuse."
ANS: BRANDO.

8) Why did Clark Gable, as Rhett Butler, in "Gone With the Wind," say, "Frankly my dear, I don't give a damn?"
ANS: SCARLETT HAD ASKED HIM WHAT WAS GOING TO HAPPEN TO HER.

9) When Judy Garland, as Dorothy, said "Toto, I've got a feeling we're not in Kansas anymore," where were they?
ANS: IN THE LAND OF OZ.

10) What actor did Mae West ask, "Why don't you come up sometime and see me?"
ANS: CARY GRANT.

JACK NICHOLSON

11) What was Clint Eastwood's name in "Sudden Impact" when he said, "Go ahead, make my day?"
ANS: HARRY CALLAHAN.

12) What was the first movie in which Sean Connery said, "Bond. James Bond."
ANS: "DR. NO."

13) When Humphrey Bogart said, "Louis, I think this is the beginning of a beautiful friendship," what actor was he talking to?
ANS: CLAUDE RAINS.

GROUCHO MARX

14) Sidney Poitier said, "They call me Mr. Tibbs." What was Mr. Tibbs' first name?
ANS: VIRGIL.

15) "Ratso" Rizzo said, "I'm walking here! I'm walking here!" Who played "Ratso?"
ANS: DUSTIN HOFFMAN.

16) What was Colin Clive referring to when he said, "It's alive! It's alive!"
ANS: THE FRANKENSTEIN *MONSTER.*

17) What actress said, "What a dump?"
ANS: BETTE DAVIS IN "BEYOND THE FOREST."

18) What was unique about the film in which Al Jolson

TALULAH BANKHEAD

PETER O'TOOLE

said, "You ain't heard nothing yet?"
ANS: IT WAS THE FIRST TALKIE. "THE JAZZ SINGER" IN 1927.

19) Who was James Cagney playing when he said, "My mother thanks you, my father thanks you and I thank you?"
ANS: GEORGE M. COHAN.

20) What line described Warren Beatty's, as Clive Barrow, job description in "Bonnie and Clyde?"

ANS: "WE ROB BANKS."

21) Brandon de Wilde called "Shane, Shane. Come back!" Who played Shane?
ANS: ALAN LADD.

22) Why did Joe E. Brown say to Jack Lemmon, "Well, nobody's perfect!"
ANS: BECAUSE LEMMON TOLD BROWN HE WAS A MAN AND NOT A WOMAN.

23) Rene Zellweger said, "You had me at 'hello'" in what film?
ANS: "JERRY MAGUIRE."

24) Groucho said it – in what movie? "One morning I shot an elephant in my pajamas. How he got in my pajamas, I don't know."
ANS: "ANIMAL CRACKERS."

25) Who said, "I'm king of the

JIMMY DURANTE

world?"
ANS: LEONARDO DI CAPRIO IN
"TITANIC."

JOE E. BROWN

26) To whom did Humphrey Bogart say, "We'll always have Paris?"
a) Lauren Bacall b) Bette Davis c) Ann Sheridan
d) Ingrid Bergman
ANS: D

27) In what film did Peter O'Toole say, "I'm not an actor, I'm a star!"
ANS: "MY FAVORITE YEAR."

28) "When the legend becomes fact, print the legend," is from what movie?
ANS: "THE MAN WHO SHOT LIBERTY VALANCE."

29) While standing next to an elephant, Jimmy Durante said, "Elephant? What elephant?" in what movie?

STAN LAUREL

ANS: "JUMBO."

30) In "On the Waterfront," who was Marlon Brando speaking to when he said, "You don't understand! I coulda had class. I coulda been a contender. I could've been somebody, instead of a bum, which is what I am."
ANS: TO HIS BROTHER, PLAYED BY ROD STEIGER.

31) What was Humphrey Bog-

DUSTIN HOFFMAN

art holding when he said, "The stuff that dreams are made of."

ANS: "THE MALTESE FALCON," 1941.

32) "I love the smell of napalm in the morning" is from what film?

ANS: "APOCALYPSE NOW," 1979.

33) What character said, "Leave the gun, take the connoli" in "The Godfather?"
a) Luca Brazzi b) Barzini c) Clemenza d) Tessio

ANS: C

34) What actor spoke the lines, "I'm mad as hell and I'm not going to take this anymore!" in "Network?" 1976.

ANS: PETER FINCH.

35) What was the song in "Casablanca" (1942) that Sam was asked to play? "Play it, Sam..."

ANS: "AS TIME GOES BY."

36) Lauren Bacall said it to Humphrey Bogart in what film? "You know how to whistle, don't you, Steve? You just put your lips together and blow."

ANS: "TO HAVE AND HAVE NOT," 1944.

37) What three words became

RONALD REAGAN

Arnold Schwarzenegger's signature line from "The Terminator" 1984?
ANS: "I'LL BE BACK."

38) Who was it Gary Cooper was portraying when he said, "Today, I consider myself the luckiest man on the face of the earth."
ANS: BASEBALL STAR LOU GEHRIG IN "PRIDE OF THE YANKEES," 1942.

KEVIN COSTNER

39) "Greed, for lack of a better word, is good," is from what film?
ANS: "WALL STREET," 1987.

40) Who said, "Well, here's another nice mess you've gotten me into?"
ANS: OLIVER HARDY TO STAN LAUREL IN "SONS OF THE DESERT," 1933.

41) Who said it in "The Shining" — "Here's Johnny!"
ANS: JACK NICHOLSON.

42) "There's no crying in baseball," is from what movie?
ANS: "A LEAGUE OF THEIR OWN," 1992.

43) Dustin Hoffman said it in "The Graduate:" "Mrs. Robinson, you're trying to seduce me. Aren't you?" Who played Mrs. Robinson?
ANS: ANN BANCROFT.

MEL BROOKS

PETER SELLERS   GINGER ROGERS

44) Who was actor Ronald Reagan speaking to when he said, "Tell them to go out there with all they've got and win just one for The Gipper."
ANS: PAT O'BRIEN, PORTRAYING COACH KNUTE ROCKNE.

45) Who was The Wicked Witch going to "get" when she said, "I'll get you, my pretty, and your little dog, too!"
ANS: DOROTHY (JUDY GARLAND) AND TOTO, IN "THE WIZARD OF OZ" 1939.

46) "I'll have what she's having," is from what film?
ANS: "WHEN HARRY MET SALLY" 1989.

47) When he was told, "Build it and they will come," what was Kevin Costner supposed to build in "Field of Dreams," 1989?
ANS: A BASEBALL FIELD.

48) "Keep your friends close but your enemies closer" was advised in what film?
ANS: "THE GODFATHER II" 1974.

49) "Elementary, my dear Watson." What actor

GLORIA SWANSON

VIVIEN LEIGH

first said it and in what film?
ANS: BASIL RATHBONE IN "THE ADVENTURES OF SHERLOCK HOLMES" 1939.

50) This exchange is from what movie: "Striker: Surely, you can't be serious. Rumack: I am serious...and don't call me Shirley."
ANS: "AIRPLANE!" 1980.

51) Who said, in "42nd Street" (1933), "It must have been tough on your mother, not having any children."
a) Ruby Keeler b) Bebe Daniels c) Una Merkel d) Ginger Rogers
ANS: D

52) Jean Hagen said it in what

ANN BANCROFT

movie? "What do you think I am? Dumb or somethin'? Why, I make more money than — than, than Calvin Coolidge! Put together!"
ANS: "SINGIN' IN THE RAIN" (1952).

53) Who said, "It's good to be the king!" in "History of the World, Part 1?"
ANS: MEL BROOKS.

CLINT EASTWOOD

54) Which of the Marx Brothers said it in "A Night at the Opera?" "You can't fool me! There ain't no sanity clause!"
a) Chico b) Harpo c) Groucho d) Zeppo
ANS: A

55) In what movie did Peter Sellers say, "Gentlemen, you can't fight in here. This is the War Room."
ANS: "DR. STRANGELOVE: OR HOW I LEARNED TO STOP WORRYING AND LOVE THE BOMB" (1964).

56) What movie is this from: "Kid, the next time I say, 'Let's go some place like Bolivia, let's go some place like Bolivia.'"
ANS: "BUTCH CASSIDY AND THE SUNDANCE KID."

57) Forest Gump was the character who said, "My mama always said life was like a box of chocolates. You never know what you're gonna get." What actor played Gump?

LAUREN BACALL

ANS: TOM HANKS.

Music & Scores

1) Vangelis composed the music for the award winning "Chariots of Fire." Which of the following is another film he wrote the music for?
a) "Chocolat" b) "Blade Runner" c) "The Black Stallion" d) "Avalon"
ANS: B

2) Was it John Barry or John Williams who did the score for "Born Free?"
ANS: JOHN BARRY.

3) The University of Southern California adapted what score from what movie as one of its fight songs? Who wrote it?
ANS: "CONQUEST" (BY ALFRED NEWMAN) FROM "CAPTAIN FROM CASTILE."

4) One of these movie scores was not written by Dimitri

JOHN WILLIAMS

MITZI GAYNOR

Tiomkin.
a) "The Alamo" b) "Dial M for Murder" c) "Duel in the Sun" d) "Viva Zapata"
ANS: D

5) Interestingly, two movies whose first word in the title was "How" had scores written by Alfred Newman. What were those movies?
ANS: "HOW THE WEST WAS WON" AND "HOW GREEN WAS MY VALLEY."

6) This composer had "In" for the first word in two of his films – "In Cold Blood" and "In the Heat of the Night." Who was he?
ANS: QUINCY JONES.

7) Which of the following films was not scored by Henry Mancini?
a) "Gunn" b) "Wait Until Dark" c) "Touch of Evil" d) "As Good As It Gets"
ANS: D

8) What was the only instrument composer Anton Karas used in "The Third Man?"
ANS: THE ZITHER.

9) True or False: Nino Rota not only wrote the music for "Godfather I" and "II", but also for "War and Peace."
ANS: TRUE.

10) Which of these Max

QUINCY JONES

Steiner-scored films came first?
a) "Gone With the Wind" b)
"The Informer" c) "Adventures
of Don Juan" d) "Casablanca"
ANS: B (1935).

11) Who wrote the theme music
for "The Sting?"
ANS: SCOTT JOPLIN.

12) Who was the on-screen
orchestra conductor in
"Fantasia?"
ANS: LEOPOLD STOKOWSKI.

SHIRLEY BASSEY

13) What Latin conductor and his orchestra
appeared in several musicals?
ANS: XAVIER CUGAT.

14) Cole Porter's last film scoring credit was for:
a) "High Society" b) "Les Girls" c) "Adam's Rib"
ANS: B, 1957.

RICHARD RODGERS

15) Who composed the "Star
Wars" theme?
ANS: JOHN WILLIAMS.

16) The score for Charlie
Chaplin's last American film,
Limelight," (1952) was com-
posed by:
ANS: CHAPLIN HIMSELF.

17) Who sang all the nominated songs for the 1965 Academy Awards?
a) Bing Crosby b) Barbra

AUDREY HEPBURN

Streisand c) Robert Goulet
d) Frank Sinatra
ANS: C

18) What was the first year
the Academy gave out an
award for Best Original Song?
a) 1940 b) 1929 c) 1945 d) 1934
ANS: D

19) Who got the Academy to
change it rule so that only
songs that are "original and
written specifically for the motion picture" are eligible to
win?
a) Cole Porter b) Jerome Kern c) Frank Sinatra
d) Oscar Hammerstein
ANS: B

20) What was the first original song to win an
Academy Award?
a) "Lullaby of Broadway" b) "The Continental"
c) "42nd Street" d) "The Way
You Look Tonight"
ANS: B

21) These four musicians are
tied for winning the most
awards for best original song,
at four. Who has had the most
nominations?
a) Alan Menken b) Jimmy Van
Heusen c) Sammy Cahn
d) Johnny Mercer
ANS: C, SAMMY CAHN WITH 26.

BING CROSBY

22) Who was the soprano among the Andrews Sisters?
ANS: MAXENE.

23) True or False: Mitzi Gaynor's real singing voice was used in her role of Nellie Forbush in "South Pacific."
ANS: TRUE.

24) What is unique about the tunes "Seventy-Six Trombones" and "Goodnight My Someone" from "The Music Man."

HENRY MANCINI

ANS: THEY ARE THE SAME MELODY, ONLY "GOODNIGHT MY SOMEONE" IS IN WALTZ TIME, "SEVENTY-SIX TROMBONES" IS A MARCH.

25) Who sang "Goldfinger" during the titles of that James Bond film?
ANS: SHIRLEY BASSEY.

26) This song, dating back to 1929, was used for the sixth time in 1952 when it became the title for this movie:
ANS: "SINGIN' IN THE RAIN."

27) What orchestra did Leopold Stokowski conduct in the 1940 version of "Fantasia?"
a) Boston Pops b) New York Philharmonic c) Philadelphia Orchestra d) Chicago Symphony
ANS: C

JEROME KERN

28) Who wrote, "Chim Chim Cher-ee" for "Mary Poppins?"
ANS: THE SHERMAN BROTHERS, ROBERT B. AND RICHARD M.

29) With the Gershwin brothers, who wrote the music and who wrote the lyrics?
ANS: GEORGE WROTE THE MUSIC, IRA WROTE THE LYRICS.

30) Who did Richard Rodgers collaborate with prior to Oscar Hammerstein II?
ANS: LORENZ HART.

LIZA MINNELLI

31) Of the following film musicals, which one did not originate on the stage?
a) "A Chorus Line" b) "Carousel" c) "Gigi" d) "My Fair Lady"
ANS: C

32) Several artists have multiple songs on AFI's list of the greatest 100 American movies music. Who has the most?
a) Barbra Streisand b) Bing Crosby c) Gene Kelly d) Judy Garland
ANS: D (JUDY HAS 5, BARBRA AND GENE 4, BING 3.)

33) Who actually sang "Moon River" in "Breakfast at Tiffany's?"
ANS: AUDREY HEPBURN DID HER OWN SINGING. SHE WAS NOT DUBBED.

MAURICE CHEVALIER

34) Judy Garland and Barbra Streisand sang songs on AFI's

COLE PORTER

list of the 100 best from different versions of the same movie title. What was it?
ANS: "A STAR IS BORN," JUDY IN 1954, BARBRA IN 1976.

35) Who are the only mother and daughter to have numbers on the AFI list of 100 greatest movie music?
ANS) JUDY GARLAND HAS FIVE SONGS ON THE LIST, HER DAUGHTER, LIZA MINELLI, HAS TWO.

36) Who sang "Thank Heaven for Little Girls" in "Gigi?"
ANS: MAURICE CHEVALIER.

37) This soprano seldom appeared on screen, but her voice was well known as she dubbed the singing of stars ranging from Natalie Wood to Sophia Loren. Who was she?
ANS: MARNI NIXON.

38) He composed the theme music for the Batman television series and for the 1968 movie and the subsequent TV series, "The Odd Couple." Name him.
a) Bill Conti b) Neal Hefti c) Henry Mancini d) Victor Young
ANS: B

39) The AFI lists "Over the Rainbow" as the top movie song of all time. Who sang the song and in what film?
ANS: JUDY GARLAND IN "THE WIZARD OF OZ."

LEOPOLD STOKOWSKI

Real Names and Reel Names

1) This Oscar-winning movie icon mostly portrayed rugged western characters, but his real name could be confused with that of a woman's. What was his real name and his reel name?
ANS: MARION MORRISON – JOHN WAYNE.

CAROL LOMBARD

2) She co-starred with all the top leading men of her time, from Clark Gable and Cary Grant to Frank Sinatra and Rock Hudson. What was her real name and her reel name?
ANS: DORIS KAPPELHOFF – DORIS DAY.

3) Was it a coincidence that her title character in this movie had her real last name? Only Woody Allen knows. What is her reel name and her

real name?
ANS: DIANE KEATON – DIANE HALL
(MOVIE: "ANNIE HALL").

4) John Charles Carter is not
a bad real name. But what did
this actor change it to?
ANS: CHARLTON HESTON.

5) Which one of the Marx
Brothers real first name was
Julius?
ANS: GROUCHO.

JACK BENNY

6) About the only thing Ice T
kept from his real name was
the T. What is his real name?
a) Tom Williams b) Tracy Morrow c) Tim McManus
ANS: B

7) Joan Fontaine has a sister who is a famous actress. What is their real last name?
ANS: DE HAVILLAND.

LIZABETH SCOTT

8) Margaret Mary Emily Ann
Hyra shortened her real name
to what reel name?
ANS: MEG RYAN.

9) Michael J. Fox's middle
name is?
a) Andrew b) John c) William
d) James
ANS: A

10) This actor was pretty
much forced to abandon his
real name, which was already

LUCILLE BALL

taken, so he went from what to what?
ANS: FROM JAMES STEWART TO STEWART GRANGER.

11) Lucy Johnson is not a bad stage name. But she changed it to what for her reel name?
a) Alice Faye b) Lucille Ball c) Ava Gardner d) Lana Turner
ANS: C

12) Nicolas Cage shares the real last name of what award-winning director?
ANS: FRANCIS FORD COPPOLA. (CAGE'S UNCLE.)

13) Frank Cooper used the name of a town in northern Indiana for his reel first name. What was it?
ANS: GARY.

14) This actor gained fame as a frightening film monster. His real name of William Henry Pratt was less imposing. Who was he?
a) Bela Lugosi b) Lon Chaney Sr. c) Boris Karloff d) Peter Cushing
ANS: C

15) Albert Einstein – not the scientist – became:
a) Eddie Albert b) Albert Brooks c) Albert Dekker d) Alfred Drake
ANS: B

NATALIE WOOD

16) Possibly Jane Peters thought her real name was too plain, because she changed it to:
a) Dorothy Lamour b) Carol Lombard c) Anne Bancroft d) Jane Russell
ANS: B

17) One of the Gumm Sisters, Frances, went on to become famous as:
ANS: JUDY GARLAND.

STEFANIE POWERS

18) This actress listed two real names – Norma Jean Mortenson and Norma Jean Baker. What was her reel name?
ANS: MARILYN MONROE.

19) Martin Sheen and Charlie Sheen share what real last name?

ANS: ESTEVEZ. CHARLIE WAS CARLOS IRWIN ESTEVEZ, MARTIN WAS RAMON ESTEVEZ.

20) Frederick Austerlitz became better known as:
a) Fredric March b) Fred Astaire c) Fred Allen d) Fred MacMurray
ANS: B

21) She kept her real first name but she changed her last name, Gustafsson, to:
ANS: GARBO.

OLIVIA DE HAVILLAND

22) Which of these three Genes – Gene Hacknan, Gene Wilder and Gene Ween – real name is Jerome Silberman?
ANS: GENE WILDER.

23) Hedwig Eva Maria Kiesler became better known by what reel name?
ANS: HEDY LAMARR.

24) Phyllis Lee Isley chose what as her reel name?
a) Joan Crawford b) Jennifer Jones c) Jayne Mansfield d) Terry Moore
ANS: B

JULIE ANDREWS

25) Michael John Douglas is his real name. For acting roles he chose to use:
a) Kirk Douglas b) Michael Caine c) Michael Keaton d) Tom Hanks
ANS: C

DON AMECHE

26) He changed his real name of Arthur Leonard Rosenberg to what reel name?
ANS: TONY RANDALL.

27) Comedian Benjamin Kubelsky oftentimes joked about the movies he made, but they were much better than he said they were. Of course, he did them under his stage name, which was:
a) George Burns b) Red Skel-

ton c) Jack Benny d) Fred Allen

ANS: C

28) This actor changed his real name, Walter Matuschan-skayasky, if for no other reason it would be hard to fit onto a theater marquee. Who was he?
a) Walter Pidgeon b) Walter Matthau c) Walter Abel
d) Dan Duryea

ANS: B

GENE WILDER

29) He was one of filmdom's leading character actors, with a broad spectrum of credits, but not under his real name, which was Laszlo Lowenstein.
a) Edward Everett Horton b) Eugene Palette c) Sidney Greenstreet d) Peter Lorre

ANS: D

EDWARD G. ROBINSON

30) What's wrong with Julia Wells as a stage name? Actually, nothing, but this actress chose not to use it even though it was her real name.
a) Julie Andrews b) Ellen Burstyn c) Jean Arthur
d) Angie Dickinson

ANS: A

31)) Brad Pitt's real name is:
a) John Bradley Pitt b) William Pittman c) William Bradley Pitt d) Brad Peters

ANS: C

MICKEY ROONEY

32) The closest to her real name of Natalia Nikolaevna Zakharenko was her first name. What was her reel name?
ANS: NATALIE WOOD.

33) Keaton is a popular name for motion picture actors. Are Buster Keaton, Michael Keaton and Diane Keaton related?
ANS: NO. ONLY BUSTER'S LAST NAME WAS KEATON. MICHAEL'S IS DOUGLAS, DIANE'S IS HALL.

34) She was of Russian heritage and her real name was Emma Matzo, which was nothing close to her reel name.
ANS: LISABETH SCOTT.

35) He started performing under his real name of Joe Yule Jr. and had the longest career in film history — but it was under his stage name. Who was he?
ANS: MICKEY ROONEY.

36) She wrote in her autobiography that her real Polish last name is Federkiewicz, but that's not close to the stage name she is known by.
a) Angela Lansbury
b) Stefanie Powers c) Suzanne Pleshette d) Cyd Charisse
ANS) B

37) She's not releated to the baby food company but Mitzi

DIANE KEATON

BORIS KARLOFF

Gaynor's real last name is?
ANS: GERBER

38) While she used her real name as an actress and comedienne, few people knew that her middle name was the exotic sounding "Desiree."
a) Cindy Williams b) Lucile Ball c) Carol Burnett d) Carol Lombard
ANS: B

39) MGM officials determined that this handsome actor's real name of Spangler Arlington Brugh had to be shortened to something more workable.
ANS: ROBERT TAYLOR.

40) He didn't make a major change from his birth name of Dominic Felix Amici, but he nonetheless simplified it a bit.
ANS: DON AMECHE.

41) He gained fame early in his movie career for his portrayal of title role in "Little Caesar." He real name was Emanuel Goldenberg. What was his stage name?
ANS: EDWARD G. ROBINSON.

42) Her real name was Vivian Mary Hartley. She kept part of it with a spelling change. Who was she?
ANS: VIVIEN LEIGH

43) This star of "Spartacus"

KIRK DOUGLAS

changed his real name from Issur Danielovitch to what?
ANS: KIRK DOUGLAS.

44) She's known by only one name, but she really does have two — Cherilyn Sarkisian. Who is she?
a) Madonna b) Beyonce c) Cher d) Elvira
ANS: CHER.

EMMY ROSSUM

45) His real name was Burle Ivanhoe but he opted to change it to a shorter version.
ANS: BURL IVES.

46) Emmy Rossum kept her last name but did some work on her real first name, which was?
a) Emily b) Emmanuelle c) Amy d) Ernestine
ANS: B

47) She discarded parts of her real name of Del-loreese Patricia Early to become?
ANS: DELLA REESE.

TONY RANDALL

48) Michael Shalhoub changed his name to one that was much more in keeping with his image as an Egyptian leading man.
ANS: OMAR SHARIF.

49) Geena Davis kept her real last name but reworked her first name, which was?
a) Regina b) Virginia c) Leena d) Angelica
ANS: B

Match the Song
to the Movie

Song: America
Movie:
(1) Patton
(2) Apocalypse Now
(3) Yankee Doodle Dandy
(4) West Side Story
ANS: 4

Song: Ol' Man River
Movie:
(1) On the Town
(2) Show Boat
(3) 42nd Street
(4) The Band Wagon
ANS: 2

Song: Stayin' Alive
Movie:
(1) Cabaret
(2) Grease

(3) Saturday Night Fever
(4) Hair
ANS: 3

Song: Some Day My Prince Will Come
Movie:
(1) Enchanted
(2) Snow White and the 7 Dwarfs
(3) Mary Poppins
(4) 101 Dalmatians
ANS: 2

Song: Moon River
Movie:
(1) Singin' in the Rain
(2) My Fair Lady
(3) Breakfast at Tiffany's
(4) The Way We Were
ANS: 3

Song: Don't Rain on My Parade
Movie:
(1) Funny Girl
(2) Fame
(3) Summer Stock
(4) Grease
ANS: 1

Song: Masquerade
Movie:
(1) Road to Morocco
(2) Cabaret
(3) Beauty and the Beast
(4) The Phantom of the Opera
ANS: 4

Song: Rock Around the Clock
Movie:

(1) Nashville
(2) Jailhouse Rock
(3) Blackboard Jungle
(4) Swing Time
ANS: 3

Song: The Windmills of Your Mind
Movie:
(1) The Thomas Crown Affair
(2) The Bodyguard
(3) Ghost
(4) Days of Wine and Roses
ANS: 1

Song: Cheek to Cheek
Movie:
(1) Swing Time
(2) Shall We Dance
(3) Top Hat
(4) Cover Girl
ANS: 3

Song: Wind Beneath My Wings
Movie:
(1) Beaches
(2) New York, New York
(3) The Way We Were
(4) Cover Girl
ANS: 1

Song: Hakuna Matata
Movie:
(1) South Pacific
(2) The Lion King
(3) Road to Morocco
(4) Tarzan
ANS: 2

Song: On the Good Ship Lollipop
Movie:
(1) The Wizard of Oz
(2) Pinocchio
(3) Bright Eyes
(4) The Muppet Movie
ANS: 3

Song: Supercalifragilisticexpialidocious
Movie:
(1) Dear Heart
(2) Mary Poppins
(3) My Kind of Town
(4) Where Love Has Gone
ANS: 2

Song: Raindrops Keep Fallin' on My Head
Movie:
(1) True Grit
(2) The Sterile Cuckoo
(3) Butch Cassidy and the Sundance Kid
(4) The Happy Ending
ANS: 3

Song: Say You, Say Me
Movie:
(1) White Nights
(2) The Color Purple
(3) A Chorus Line
(4) Back to the Future
ANS: 1

Song: Sooner or Later
Movie:
(1) The Godfather Part III
(2) Home Alone
(3) Young Guns II
(4) Dick Tracy

ANS: 4

Song: Streets of Philadelphia
Movie:
(1) Sleepless in Seattle
(2) Poetic Justice
(3) The Philadelphia Story
(4) Philadelphia
ANS: 4

Song: You'll Be in My Heart
Movie:
(1) Music of the Heart
(2) Tarzan
(3) Toy Story 2
(4) Magnolia
ANS: 2

Song: You Must Love Me
Movie:
(1) Evita
(?) Phantom of the Opera
(3) Up Close and Personal
(4) The Mirror Has Two Faces
ANS: 1

Song: Falling Slowly
Movie:
(1) Enchanted
(2) August Rush
(3) Once
(4) Dreamgirls
ANS: 3

Song: We Belong Together
Movie:
(1) Tangled
(2) Country Strong

(3) Toy Story 3
(4) Nine
ANS: 3

Song: Let It Go
Movie:
(1) Despicable Me 2
(2) Her
(3) The Lego Movie
(4) Frozen
ANS: 4

Song: Writing's on the Wall
Movie:
(1)) Spectre
(2) Begin Again
(3) Racing Extinction
(4) The Hunting Ground
ANS: 1

Song: Thanks For the Memory
Movie:
(1) That Certain Age
(2) The Big Broadcast of 1938
(3) The Lady Objects
(4) Alexander's Ragtime Band
ANS: 2

Song: Begin the Beguine
Movie:
(1) Top Hat
(2) Down Argentine Way
(3) Three Little Words
(4) Broadway Melody of 1940
ANS: 4

Sports

1) What prize fighter did Paul Newman portray in "Someboy Up There Likes Me?"
ANS: ROCKY GRAZIANO.

2) Who played Jim Thorpe in "Jim Thorpe, All American?"
ANS: BURT LANCASTER.

3) What college team did Jim Thorpe play for?
ANS: CARLISLE INDIANS.

BABE RUTH

4) Babe Ruth has been played by William Bendix and John Goodman. Who played him in "Pride of the Yankees."
ANS: THE BABE PLAYED HIMSELF.

5) In which of the following sports films was the hero fictional?
a) "Fear Strikes Out" b) "The

Natural" c) "Raging Bull"
d) "Rudy"
ANS: B

6) Two films have been made about the racehorse, Seabiscuit. What child star appeared in the first one?
ANS: SHIRLEY TEMPLE.

7) The Marx Brothers made at least two sports comedies – "A Day at the Races" and "Horsefeathers." Were both about horse racing?
ANS: NO. "HORSEFEATHERS" WAS ABOUT FOOTBALL.

GARY COOPER
AS LOU GEHRIG

8) Name three different sports in three different films that Paul Newman engaged in.
ANS: HOCKEY IN "SLAPSHOT," POOL IN "THE HUSTLER," BOXING IN "SOMEBODY UP THERE LIKE ME."

9) Besides having played Tarzan in the movies, what else do these actors have in common — Johnny Weissmuller, Buster Crabbe, Bruce Bennett and Glenn Morris?
ANS: ALL WERE OLYMPIC GAMES ATHLETES.

10) Who played Jackie Robinson in "The Jackie Robinson Story?"
ANS: ROBINSON PLAYED HIMSELF.

11) Sean Astin played football for Notre Dame in what movie?
ANS: "RUDY."

ANTHONY PERKINS

PAT O'BRIEN AND RONALD REAGAN IN "KNUTE ROCKNE-ALL AMERICAN"

12) "Gentleman Jim," "Rocky" and "The Great White Hope" were about heavyweight boxers. What differentiates the films?
ANS: "ROCKY" WAS A FICTITIOUS CHARACTER. THE OTHERS WERE ABOUT REAL PEOPLE.

13) What was the sport portrayed in "Chariots of Fire?"
ANS: TRACK.

14) In the 1925 movie "The Freshman" he was a football player. Who was he?
ANS: HAROLD LLOYD.

15) Which one of these was not a boxing movie?
a) "The Harder They Fall" b) "Fists of Fury" c) "The Cinderella Man" d) "Creed"
ANS: B (MARTIAL ARTS).

16) Sylvester Stallone gained fame as a boxer in "Rocky." In what movie did he participate in another sport?
ANS: "VICTORY" (SOCCER).

17) Burt Reynolds played football in "The Longest Yard." Name another movie in which he played the game.

PAUL NEWMAN

SHIRLEY TEMPLE

ANS: "SEMI-TOUGH."

18) What was the sport where Tom Cruise put on "All the Right Moves?"
ANS: FOOTBALL.

19) Who played golfer Ben Hogan in "Follow the Sun?"
ANS: GLENN FORD.

20) Robert DeNiro played a catcher in "Bang the Drum Slowly." Who played the pitcher?
ANS: MICHAEL MORIARTY.

21) Burt Lancaster went from football in "Jim Thorpe All American" to what sport in what movie?
ANS: BASEBALL IN "FIELD OF DREAMS."

22) What was the sport in "Million Dollar Baby?"
ANS: BOXING.

23) Kevin Costner has been in baseball and football-themed movies. Name a movie he was in that covered a sport other than those two.
ANS: "TIN CUP" – GOLF.

24) Who played boxer Jake LaMotta in "The Raging Bull," 1980?
a) Paul Newman b) Sylvester Stallone c) Robert DeNiro
d) Steve McQueen
ANS: C

GLENN FORD

JACKIE ROBINSON

25) James Caan was a football player in "Brian's Song." What was his sport in "Rollerball?"
ANS: A FUTURISTIC ROLLER DERBY.

26) What was the sport in "Talladega Nights: The Ballad of Ricky Bobby?"
ANS: AUTO RACING.

27) What was Sonja Henie's claim to fame before she became an actress?
ANS: SHE WAS AN ICE SKATER.

28) Who played the team owner in "Any Given Sunday?"
a) Cameron Diaz b) Jamie Fox c) James Woods
d) Al Pacino
ANS: A

29) Which one of the following actors did not play a coach in a movie?
a) Al Pacino b) John Wayne
c) Gene Hackman d) Robert Duvall
ANS: D

30) What future governor did Lou Ferrigno co-star with in "Pumping Iron?"
a) George Murphy b) Ronald Reagan c) Arnold Schwarzenegger d) Charlton Heston
ANS: C

ROBERT DE NIRO

31) What is the topic of "The

BURT REYNOLDS

Endless Summer?"
ANS: SURFING.

32) Who played Muhammed Ali in the 2001 movie, "Ali?"
ANS: WILL SMITH.

33) What is the movie about bowling in which Bill Murray and Woody Harrelson are adversaries?
ANS: "KINGPIN." 1996.

34) Prison inmates play football against their guards in what movie?
ANS: "THE LONGEST YARD."

35) What is the sport in "Victory?"
ANS: SOCCER.

36) In 1979's "Heaven Can Wait," what sport and what position did Warren Beatty play?
ANS: FOOTBALL – QUARTERBACK.

37) Anthony Perkins played Jimmy Piersall in the movie version of "Fear Strikes Out." Who played Piersall in the TV version?
a) Tab Hunter b) Troy Donahue c) Warren Beatty d) Tom Hanks
ANS: A

38) What was the game Auric Goldfinger played in "Goldfin-

HAROLD LLOYD

ger?"
ANS: GOLF.

39) Which one of these actors did not appear in "Caddyshack?"
a) Rodney Dangerfield b) Dan Ackroyd c) Chevy Chase d) Bill Murray
ANS: B

40) What sporting event is featured in the "Ascot Gavotte" number in "My Fair Lady?"
ANS: HORSE RACING.

SONJA HENIE

41) What university was "Knute Rockne-All American" coaching when "The Gipper" was on his team?
ANS: NOTRE DAME.

42) What sport was used to pull off the sting in the movie of the same name?
a) Football b) Baseball c) Horse Racing d) Ice Hockey
ANS: C

43) All the following appeared in the movie, but who played boxer Toro Moreno in "The Harder They Fall" (1956)?
a) Mike Lane b) Max Baer c) Jersey Joe Walcott d) Carlos Montalban
ANS: A

44) What was the sport in "The Color of Money?" (1986).
ANS: POOL.

BILL MURRAY

The Crew

1) The crew member who usually calls for "Quiet on the Set" is:
a) The Director b) The Sound Man c) The Assistant Director
ANS: C

2) The movie producer's executive officer and right hand man is usually:
a) The Cinematographer b) The Director c) The Unit Manager
ANS: C

3) The Gaffer is the film unit's:
a) Chief Electrician b) Assistant Editor c) Boom Operator
ANS: A

4) The Continuity Person is also known as
ANS: THE SCRIPT SUPERVISOR.

5) The Lead Man is:
ANS: FOREMAN OF THE SET'S CREW.

6) Who does the Director generally work with in determining how he wants the film to look and be lit?
ANS: THE DIRECTOR OF PHOTOGRAPHY.

7) What does the Loader do?
ANS: HE LOADS RAW FILM INTO THE FILM MAGAZINES.

8) Who is the Boom Operator's immediate boss?
ANS: THE PRODUCTION SOUND MIXER.

9) What does the Key Grip do?
ANS: HEADS THE SET OPERATIONS DEPARTMENT.

10) What is a Best Boy?
ANS: CHIEF ASSISTANT TO THE KEY GRIP OR THE GAFFER.

11) Who does the Negative Cutter report to?
ANS: THE FILM EDITOR.

12) The Foley Artist does what?
ANS: RECORDS MANY OF THE SOUND EFFECTS FOR THE FILM.

13) If the Composer writes the music score for a film, what does the Music Supervisor or Music Director do?
ANS: WORKS WITH COMPOSER, MIXERS AND EDITORS TO CREATE AND INTEGRATE THE FILM'S MUSIC.

14) Who is responsible for creating the physical and visual appearance of the film?
ANS: THE PRODUCTION DESIGNER.

15) Who is the number two person in the set department, just below the Set Decorator?
ANS: THE BUYER.

The Silents

1) True or False – After director D. W. Griffith finished filming battle scenes for "Birth of A Nation" in 1915 in what is now Griffith Park, he donated the land for the Los Angeles park.
ANS: FALSE. THE LAND WAS DONATED BY COL. GRIFFITH J. GRIFFITH IN 1896.

CHARLIE CHAPLIN

2) She has been called the most popular star in screen history and America's sweetheart. Name her.
ANS: MARY PICKFORD.

3) Who were the "united artists" who formed a studio of that name?
ANS: MARY PICKFORD, DOUGLAS FAIRBANKS SR. AND CHARLIE CHAPLIN.

4) Before motion pictures

D. W. GRIFFITH   MACK SENNETT

made the small hamlet of Hollywood famous, it was better known for:
a) Its cattle ranches b) Its fruit orchards c) Its vacation cottages d) Its climate
ANS: B

5) Who played Charlie Chaplin in the movie version of the comedian's life?
ANS: ROBERT DOWNEY JR.

6) Gloria Swanson, who started as a silent movie comedienne in 1915, was how old when she portrayed the faded film star Norma Desmond in "Sunset Boulevard" in 1950?
a) 53 b) 61 c) 57 d) 70
ANS: A

7) Rudolph Valentino began his movie career as:
a) Rudy Valentine b) Rodolfo de Valentina c) Ruggerio Rodolfo d) Rodolfo di Luca
ANS: B

8) Erich von Stroheim portrayed Gloria Swanson's

butler and former husband and director in "Sunset Boulevard." How had he worked with Swanson in the silents?
a) As a writer b) As a director c) As a producer d) As an actor
ANS: B

9) He was the leading producer of slapstick and comic movies and soon earned the nickname, "The King of Comedy." Who was he?
a) Charlie Chaplin b) Mack Sennett c) Col. William Selig d) Carl Laemmle
ANS: B

MARY PICKFORD

10) What movie started as a silent but is credited with being the first talkie?
ANS: "THE JAZZ SINGER" STARRING AL JOLSON.

RUDOLPH VALENTINO

11) The sons and daughters of several silent film stars followed their parents into acting. Which one of the following did not?
a) Lon Chaney Jr. b) Tyrone Power c) Lillian Gish d) Douglas Fairbanks Jr.
ANS: C

12) What was the running time of the one-reeler silent screen shorts?
a) 20 minutes b) 11 minutes c) 5 minutes d) 9 minutes

ANS: B

13) Jackie the Lion appeared in
the MGM opening credits logo.
What studio owned him?
a) MGM b) Fox c) Selig
d) Vitagraph
ANS: C

14) What year was the first
movie shot in Los Angeles?
a) 1908 b) 1901 c) 1911 d) 1905
ANS: A

LILLIAN GISH

15) The first permanent film
studio in Los Angeles was located on what street?
a) Hollywood Blvd. b) Mission Road c) Allesandro
St. d) Sunset Blvd.
ANS: C

16) Fan magazines date back to the silent era.
What was the first one, which debuted in 1911?

a) Photoplay b) Motion Picture
Story Magazine c) Moving Pic-
ture World d) Motion Picture
News
ANS: B

17) Theodosia Goodman
gained fame in Fox's first feature release, "A Fool There
Was," in 1916. What was her
stage name?
a) Gloria Swanson b) Lillian
Gish c) Theda Bara d) Norma
Talmadge
COLLEEN MOORE   ANS C

FLORENCE
LAWRENCE

18) True or False: The initials in D. W. Griffith's name stand for David Ward.
ANS: FALSE. THEY STAND FOR DAVID WARK.

19) What was the name of the studio facilities Tom Mix built in the Edendale district of Los Angeles?
ANS: MIXVILLE.

20) What actor, who was to become one of the silents great comedy stars, began working in the business as an apprentice for Mack Sennett in 1913?
a) Ben Turpin b) Charlie Chaplin c) Harold Lloyd d) Buster Keaton
ANS: B

21) The top grossing film of the 1920s was:
a) "Wings" b) "The Ten Commandments" c) "Ben-

DOUGLAS FAIRBANKS
SR.

DOUGLAS FAIRBANKS
JR.

Hur" d) "The Big Parade"
ANS: D

22) What American inventor is credited with the development of early film cameras and projectors?
a) Thomas Edison b) Alexander Graham Bell c) Benjamin Franklin d) Samuel Morse
ANS: A

RONALD COLMAN

23) The world's first film production studio was completed in 1893 and, besides the Kinetographic Theater, was known as:
ANS: THE BLACK MARIA.

24) When Alice Guy Blache made a one-minute film in April of 1896 what unique position in the history of motion pictures did it earn her?
ANS. SHE BECAME THE WORLD'S FIRST FEMALE FILM DIRECTOR.

FRANCIS X. BUSHMAN

25) The first film shot specifically in Hollywood was a 1910 melodrama entitled:
a) "In Old California" b) "A California Hold-Up" c) "The Great Train Roberry" d) "Ramona"
ANS: A

26) The first, official feature length film, at least an hour in length, was the 1906 "The Story of the Kelly Gang." In what country was it made?

MABEL NORMAND   NORMA TALMADGE

a) England b) Australia c) USA d) France
ANS: B

27) Roscoe "Fatty" Arbuckle is credited with receiving the first pie in the face in a motion picture. Who threw the pie?
a) Mabel Normand b) Colleen Moore b) Florence Lawrence d) Charlie Chaplin
ANS: A

28) The Warner brothers were originally:
a) Shoe salesmen b) Junk dealers c) Soap salesmen d) Vaudeville actors
ANS: C

29) Who made the first film adaptation of "Robin Hood?"
a) D. W. Griffith b) Col. William Selig c) Carl Laemmle d) Cecil B. DeMille
ANS: C

30) D. W. Griffith's "Birth of a Nation" was the longest film made in the US at the time. What year

was it released?
a) 1919 b) 1913 c) 1915 d) 1911
ANS: C

31) Lois Webber is the first women to direct a feature length film in the US, "The Merchant of Venice." What year?
a) 1922 b) 1916 c) 1914 d) 1919
ANS: C

BUSTER KEATON

32) Besides being actors, what did the following have in common: Ramon Navarro, Francis X. Bushman, Rudolph Valentino, Clara Bow, William S. Hart and Marion Davies.
ANS: THEY WERE ALL SUPER-STARS OF THE SILENT FILM ERA.

33) While Annette Kellerman made several silent films, what was she best known for?
ANS: SHE WAS A CHAMPION SWIM-MER AND DIVER.

BEN TURPIN

34) She is credited with being the first film performer to be known to the public by name, in essence, the first "movie star." Who was she?
a) Mary Pickford b) Florence Lawrence c) Lillian Gish d) Pearl White
ANS: B

35) Charlie Chaplin introduced his "Tramp" character

CLARA BOW

in what film?
a) "Tillie's Punctured Romance" b) "The Tramp" c) "Kid Auto Races at Venice" d) "The Rink"
ANS: C

36) John Wayne began his movie career in the silent days as:
a) A stunt man b) A property man c) A horse wrangler d) A cowboy extra
ANS: B

37) It is generally considered to be the first action film and it was made in 1903. What is its title?
ANS: "THE GREAT TRAIN ROBBERY."

38) Prior to his 52 years as a director, Raoul Walsh was an actor. What was his pivotal role in "Birth of a Nation?"
a) Abraham Lincoln b) General Grant c) John Wilkes Booth d) Jefferson Davis
ANS: C

39) Who is the first movie actress to receive a percentage of her film's earnings?
a) Pola Negri b) Theda Bara
c) Clara Bow d) Mary Pickford
ANS: D

40) This silent film star is credited with discovering Gretchen Young and suggesting she change her first name to Loretta.

RAMON NAVARRO

a) Colleen Moore b) Marion Davies c) Clara Bow d) Gloria Swanson
ANS: A

41) Which of these actors was not a stock player for D. W. Griffith?
a) Lionel Barrymore b) Gary Cooper c) Donald Crisp
d) Mary Pickford
ANS: B

"FATTY" ARBUCKLE

42) When she retired she was wealthy, and it's no surprise because she was making $12,500 a week in 1927 as the top box-office draw in the US. Who was she?
a) Gloria Swanson b) Mary Pickford c) Colleen Moore d) Clara Bow
ANS: C

43) He and his family escaped to Los Angeles from the Mexican Revolution in 1913. By 1925 he was the star of "Ben-Hur." What was his name?
ANS: RAMON NAVARRO.

MARION DAVIES

44) Her role in the 1927 film, "It," gave Clara Bow a nickname that stuck with her beyond her film career. What was it?
ANS: THE "IT GIRL."

45) True or False: Norma Street in West Hollywood and Talmadge Street in Los Feliz

THOMAS EDISON

in Los Angeles were named for silent film actress, Norma Talmadge.
ANS: TRUE.

46) Although he was best known as a comedian, this silent film star was a highly regarded director who was voted the seventh greatest director of all time by one publication. Who was he?
a) Charlie Chaplin b) Harold Lloyd c) Buster Keaton d) Roscoe "Fatty" Arbuckle
ANS: C

47) He is one of the stars of the Golden Age of Hollywood, with a career that started in the silents in 1917 and included many feature films plus the lead in the television series, "The Halls of Ivy," in 1954. Name him.
ANS: RONALD COLMAN.

48) He had a career that stretched over 55 years and was the first actor to be called, "King of the Movies." Who was he?
a) Rudolph Valentino b) Francis X. Bushman
c) Ramon Navarro d) John Gilbert
ANS: B

49) He is known as the screen's first cowboy but his first credited film role was as Messala in the 1907 version of "Ben-Hur." Who was he?
a) Tom Mix b) William S. Hart c) "Broncho Billy" Anderson d) Emil Jannings
ANS: B

50) Both father and son appeared in the silents and

talkies and both were among the top stars in the business during their acting careers. Who were they?

ANS: DOUGLAS FAIRBANKS SENIOR AND JUNIOR.

51) This was a premier year for films, with such releases as "Battleship Potemkin," "Ben-Hur," "The Gold Rush" and "The Phantom of the Opera"among others. What year was it?

a) 1923 b) 1927) c) 1925 d) 1929

ANS: C

JACKIE THE LION FILMS THE MGM LOGO.

The Studios

1) The first permanent studio in Los Angeles was established in 1909 at the corner of Clifford and Allesandro Streets (now Glendale Boulevard) in the Edendale district by whom?
a) Carl Laemmle b) Mack Sennett c) Col. William Selig d) Thomas Ince
ANS: C

2) What two studios butted up against each other on Melrose Avenue in Hollywood?
ANS: PARAMOUNT AND RKO.

3) What major studio was originally located in Hollywood's "Gower Gulch?"
ANS: COLUMBIA.

4) What studio was owned for a time by Howard Hughes?
ANS: RKO.

5) What studio had a city named after it?
ANS: UNIVERSAL (CITY).

6) Irving Thalberg and Harry Cohn got their starts as secretaries at what studio?
ANS: UNIVERSAL.

7) Stars such as John Wayne, Gene Autry and Roy Rogers all made westerns for what studio?
a) Monogram b) Warner Bros. c) Republic
d) Universal
ANS: C

8) The location that until recently housed public television station KCET in Los Angeles was the original home of what studio?
a) Bison b) Monogram c) First National d) Mack Sennett
ANS: B

9) Mary Pickford, Douglas Fairbanks Sr. and Charlie Chaplin formed United Artists. What star later owned the studio?
ANS: TOM CRUISE.

10) The William Fox Studio merged with 20th Century Studio in what year to form 20th Century-Fox?

THE SELIG STUDIO AT 1845 ALLESANDRO ST.
(NOW GLENDALE BLVD.) IN THE EDENDALE
DISTRICT OF LOS ANGELES, 1909.

HARRY COHN

a) 1939 b) 1928 c) 1935
d) 1941
ANS: C

11) Who became head of MGM
when it was established in
1924?
ANS: LOUIS B. MAYER.

12) What studio that was in
Hollywood proper is now
housed on the former MGM lot
in Culver City?
ANS: COLUMBIA.

13) Originally called Samuel
Goldwyn Studios, it has undergone several name
changes and is now known as The Lot. Where is it
located?
a) Studio City b) Culver City c) West Hollywood
d) Santa Monica
ANS: C

14) What two major studios are almost neighbors in
Burbank?
ANS: WALT DISNEY AND WARNER BROS.

15) The Mack Sennett Studios made its early comedies in Los Angeles-area facilities located in:
a) Glendale b) Edendale c) Ferndell d) Lincoln Park
ANS: B

16) Before moving to Burbank, the Walt Disney
Studios were located in what Los Angeles neighbor-
hood?
a) Silver Lake b) Hollywood c) Westlake d) Lincoln
Park
ANS: A

17) What studio was housed for a while in Burbank after a move from Hollywood?
ANS: COLUMBIA.

18) Much of the land used for the Century City development in west Los Angeles was originally part of what studio?
ANS: 20TH CENTURY-FOX.

19) The first all-concrete soundstage was built by what studio?
a) Vitagraph b) MGM c) Mack Sennett d) Bison
ANS: C

20) Prior to being taken over by Warner Bros., the studio's second facility in Burbank was called:
ANS: COLUMBIA RANCH.

21) When Universal merged its studio in 1946 it became known as:
ANS: UNIVERSAL-INTERNATIONAL.

PARAMOUNT STUDIOS IN HOLLYWOOD, 1933.

LOUIS B. MAYER

22) Vitagraph was one of the successful early day studios. What company took it over in 1925?
a) MGM b) Warner Bros.
c) Universal d) Paramount
ANS: B

23) Which of the Talmadge sisters built a studio facility in east Hollywood?
a) Constance b) Norma
c) Natalie
ANS: B

24) When Samuel Goldwyn did not become part of the Metro-Goldwyn-Mayer merger, what did he do?
ANS: HE FORMED SAMUEL GOLDWYN PRODUCTIONS.

25) Carl Laemmle founded Universal Pictures in 1912. What year did he establish Universal City?
a) 1921 b) 1912 c) 1915 d) 1929
ANS: C

26) Which one of these studios is actually in Hollywood?
a) Warner Bros. b) Sony
c) Raleigh d) Walt Disney
ANS: C

27) Who were the Warner Brothers besides Jack?
ANS: HARRY, ALBERT AND SAM.

28) What famous comedian built a studio on La Brea Av-

HOWARD HUGHES

enue in Hollywood?
ANS: CHARLIE CHAPLIN.

29) Mack Sennett moved his studio from Edendale to what part of Los Angeles?
ANS: STUDIO CITY.

30) This studio, still standing at Prospect and Talmadge in the Los Felix district of Los Angeles, was originally the Vitagraph Studios. When did it open?
a) 1923 b) 1915 c) 1911 d) 1922
ANS: B

31) Two studios celebrated their 100th anniversary in 2012. Name them, the oldest one first.
ANS: PARAMOUNT AND UNIVERSAL. PARAMOUNT IS ONE MONTH OLDER.

32) Pixar's animated feature, "Brave," in 2012, was its thirteenth animated feature but its first of a kind. What was that?
ANS: IT WAS PIXAR'S FIRST FILM TO HAVE A FEMALE LEAD CHARACTER.

MACK SENNETT STUDIOS AT 1712 ALLESANDRO ST. (GLENDALE BLVD.) IN EDENDALE, LOS ANGELES, 1917.

33) What studio had these three consecutive Best Picture winners: "American Beauty," 1999, "Gladiator," 2000, "A Beautiful Mind," 2001?
a) Universal b) DreamWorks c) Lions Gate d) Miramax
ANS: B

34) Miramax Studios was formed in 1979 by?
a) Steven Spielberg b) The Weinstein Brothers c) 20th Century Fox d) Michael Eisner
ANS: B

35) What is the name of the company that Disney started to make films that appealed to an older audience?
a) Searchlight Productions b) Lions Gate c) Touchstone Pictures d) Tri-Star
ANS: C

36) What was notable about Sherry Lansing's appointment as president of production at 20th Cen-

THE BURBANK STUDIOS (WARNER BROS.), 1981.

tury-Fox Studios in 1980?
ANS: SHE BECAME THE FIRST
FEMALE TO HEAD A MAJOR STU-
DIO.

37) What beverage company
purchased Columbia Pictures
in 1982?
a) Pepsi Cola b) Seagram's
c) Nestle's d) Coca Cola
ANS: D

38) Now known as the Sony
Pictures Entertainment lot in
Culver City, what studio
owned the facility just prior to
the purchase by Sony?
ANS: MGM.

JACK WARNER

39) What studio made the Tarzan films that
starred Johnny Weismuller in the title role?
a) MGM b) Columbia c) RKO d) Republic
ANS. C

40) The chariot race in the
original "Ben-Hur," filmed in
Italy, had to be re-shot. Where
was that done?
ANS: ON THE MGM BACKLOT IN
CULVER CITY.

41) What does RKO stand for?
ANS: RADIO KEITH ORPHEUM.

42) Where was "Poverty Row,"
home to several independent
studios, located?
ANS: ON SUNSET BLVD. IN HOLLY-
WOOD, JUST SOUTH OF GOWER ST.

SHERRY LANSING

The Teams

1) Laurel and Hardy first appeared together in a silent short called "The Lucky Dog" in 1921. What year did they make their last film together?
ANS: 1952.

2) Which of these stars did not appear in a film with Laurel and Hardy?
a) Jean Harlow b) Robert Mitchum c) Peter Cushing d) Myrna Loy
ANS: D

LAUREL AND HARDY

3) The Tin Man was played in a 1925 silent version of "The Wizard of Oz" by:
a) Buster Keaton b) Oliver Hardy c) Douglas Fairbanks Sr.
d) Charlie Chaplin
ANS: B

4) The Marx Brothers made a total of 13 films

over a 20 year span.
What were those years?
a)1921-1941 b)1925-
1945 c)1930 1950
d)1929-1949
ANS: A

5) Chico, Harpo and
Groucho were the most
famous of the Marx
Brothers. But there
were two other broth-
ers. Name them.
ANS: GUMMO AND ZEPPO.

6) Who was the oldest of
the Marx Brothers?
ANS: CHICO.

THE MARX BROTHERS

7) Abbott and Costello
made a total of 36 films
together. What studio
produced the majority (28) of them?
a) RKO b) Warner Bros. c) MGM d) Universal
ANS: D

8) Which of the following actors did not appear in
an Abbott and Costello movie:
a) Charles Laughton b) Boris Karloff c) Craig
Stevens d) Buster Keaton
ANS: D

9) How long did Martin and Lewis perform as a
team?
a) 5 years b) 10 years c) 8 years d) 11 years
ANS: B

10) The first film Martin and Lewis appeared in was:
a) "My Friend Irma" b) "At War with the Army"
c) "That's My Boy"
ANS: A

11) What was Martin and Lewis' last movie together?
a) "Living It Up" b) "Pardners" c) "Hollywood or Bust"
ANS: C

12) Bob Hope and Bing Crosby made their first Road picture in what year?
a) 1940 b) 1939 c) 1944 D) 1941
ANS: A

13) What was the title of the first Road picture?
a) "Road to Singapore" b) "Road to Morocco"
c) "Road to Bali"
ANS: A

14) How many Road pictures were made?
a) 12 b) 9 c) 5 d) 7
ANS: D

ABBOTT AND COSTELLO

15) Who was the third regular star in all the Road pictures?

ANS: DOROTHY LAMOUR.

16) How many films did Fred Astaire and Ginger Rogers make together?
a)10 b) 8 c) 12 d) 6
ANS: A

17) What was the first film Fred and Ginger made together?

ANS: "FLYING DOWN TO RIO."

MARTIN AND LEWIS

18) What was the year of Fred and Ginger's first film:
a) 1934 b) 1936 c) 1933 d)1940
ANS: C

19) What was the last film made together by Fred and Ginger?
ANS: "THE BARKLEYS OF BROADWAY."

20) What was the year of their last film?
ANS: 1949.

21) How many films did Fred and Ginger make in color?
ANS: JUST ONE. THEIR LAST ONE, "THE BARKELYS OF BROADWAY."

22) What studio produced nine of the 10 Fred Astaire-Ginger Rogers movies?
a) RKO b) 20th Century Fox c) MGM d) Warner

Bros.
ANS: A

23) Ginger Rogers became the highest paid actress in Hollywood by the 1940s. Did she ever win an Academy Award?
ANS: YES. IN 1941, FOR "KITTY FOYLE."

24) Who made their movie debut first, Fred Astaire or Ginger Rogers?
ANS: GINGER IN 1929. FRED'S WAS IN 1933.

25) What was the age difference between Fred and Ginger?
a) Fred, 12 years older b) Same age c) Fred, 5 years older d) Ginger, 1 year older
ANS: A

26) What female singing group was the most imitated of all time?
a) The McGuire Sisters b) The Lennon Sisters
c) The Andrews Sisters d) The Pointer Sisters
ANS: C

27) From 1942 to 1967 Spencer Tracy and

KATHARINE HEPBURN AND SPENCER TRACY

Katharine Hepburn teamed up for how many films?
a) 5 b) 7 c) 9 d) 4
ANS: B

THE THREE STOOGES

28) Who teamed up to become "Dirty Rotten Scoundrels" in the 1988 movie of the same name?
a) Bob Hope and Bing Crosby
b) Chevy Chase and Bill Murray c) Steve Martin and Michael Caine
ANS: C

29) Who were the "Three Amigos?"
a) The Three Stooges b) Steve Martin, Chevy Chase and Martin Short c) Dan Ackroyd, Harold Ramis and Bill Murray
ANS: B

30) What were the first names of the Andrews Sisters?
ANS: PATTY, MAXENE AND LAVERNE.

31) In what Abbott and Costello film did the Andrews sisters sing their best-known song, "Boogie Woogie Bugle Boy?"
ANS: "BUCK PRIVATES."

32) Although not officially a "team," they made 13 films together, including several about private eye Nick Charles and his wife, Nora. Who were they?
ANS: WILLIAM POWELL AND MYRNA LOY.

33) Who made more films than any other singing group in Hollywood history?
ANS: THE ANDREWS SISTERS.

34) This team made 21 movies together, mostly in the 1930s, but is mostly forgotten today.
a) Morecambe and Wise b) Wheeler and Woolsey
c) Frick and Frack d) Amos and Andy
ANS: B

35) This brother team has been credited with influencing such comedians as Danny Kaye, Jerry Lewis and Sid Caesar. Who were they?
a) The Marx Brothers b) The Smothers Brothers
c) The Ritz Brothers
ANS: C

36) How many films did the three Ritz brothers make during their careers?
a) 20 b) 8 c) 12 d) 11
ANS: A

37) Over the act's run, how many actual "stooges" made up the Three Stooges team?
a) 4 b) 3 c) 8 d) 6
ANS: D

38) Which of The Three Stooges were in all the team's films?
ANS: MOE AND LARRY.

THE ANDREWS SISTERS

39) Wallace Beery and Marie Dressler teamed for a film in 1930 that has become a classic.

What is it's name?
ANS: "MIN AND BILL."

40) How many films did Basil Rathbone and Nigel Bruce make as Sherlock Holmes and Dr. Watson?
a) 9 b) 12 c) 14 d) 15
ANS: C

41) Keye Luke appeared in seven films with Warner Oland in what series?
ANS: CHARLIE CHAN.

KEYE LUKE

42) Although not officially a team, they made 10 pictures together, starting with "The Fortune Cookie" in 1966. Who were they?
ANS: JACK LEMMON AND WALTER MATTHAU.

43) Cheech and Chong's first movie was appropriately titled:

STEVE MARTIN

a) "Nice Dreams" b) "Things Are Tough All Over" c) "Up in Smoke" d) "Still Smokin"
ANS: C

44) How many "Star Trek" movies were made that teamed the original television series cast?
a) 4 b) 8 c) 6 d) 5
ANS: C

45) Ernest Borgnine and Robert Ryan teamed in another film after "The Dirty Dozen." What was it?
ANS: "THE WILD BUNCH."

The Movies

1) "His Girl Friday" was a version of what stage play which also was made into several movies under its original name?
ANS: "THE FRONT PAGE."

2) Three heavyweight boxing champions, Max Baer, Primo Carnera and Jack Dempsey, received the top male acting credits in what 1933 MGM film?
ANS: "THE PRIZEFIGHTER AND THE LADY."

3) Charles Laughton played Henry VIII in two films, one was, "The Private Life of Henry VIII," in 1933. What was the other, in 1953?
ANS: "YOUNG BESS."

4) They might better have been called "Easterns." Where were the early, silent Western films shot?
a) New York b) Florida c) Pennsylvania d) New Jersey

MARLON BRANDO AS DON VITO CORLEONE IN "THE GODFATHER I"

ROBERT DE NIRO AS DON VITO CORLEONE IN "THE GODFATHER II"

ANS: D

5) "Everybody Goes to Rick's" was the name of the play, but the movie was called what?
ANS: "CASABLANCA."

6) In what film did the son direct his actor father?
ANS: "TREASURE OF SIERRA MADRE." JOHN DIRECTED WALTER HUSTON.

7) This film ran more than three hours, yet there are no speaking roles in it for women.
ANS: "LAWRENCE OF ARABIA."

8) He wrote the novel on which this film was based and co-wrote the screenplay with director Francis Ford Coppola. Who was he and what was the name of his novel?
ANS: MARIO PUZO, "THE GODFATHER."

9) What is the Number One movie on the American

Film Institute's list of the 100 best movies of all time?
a) "The Godfather I" b) "Casablanca" c) "Citizen Kane" d) "Gone With the Wind"
ANS: C

10) The highest rated musical on the American Film Institute's list of 100 best films is ranked an overall sixth. What is it?
a) "Singin' in the Rain" b) "The Sound of Music" c) "An American in Paris" d) "The Wizard of Oz"
ANS: D

11) What movie was the story of the transition from silent films to sound and whose title song had been used in several prior films?
ANS: "SINGIN' IN THE RAIN."

12) The highest-rated comedy is Number 14 on

DONALD O'CONNOR, DEBBIE REYNOLDS AND GENE KELLY IN "SINGIN' IN THE RAIN."

AFI's list.
a) "Tootsie" b) "Some Like It Hot" c) "Duck Soup" d) "Bringing Up Baby"
ANS: B

13) Number 100 on AFI's list of 100 is what film?
a) "Goodfellas" b) "The Apartment" c) "Yankee Doodle Dandy" d) "The Searchers"
ANS: C

JEAN ARTHUR

14) Harry Lime is dead — or is he — in this intriguing film set in Vienna just after World War II.
ANS: "THE THIRD MAN."

15) Who was the future star comedian who got his first major screen role in "Bonnie and Clyde?"
ANS: GENE WILDER.

16) "The Island of Dr. Moreau," from the novel by H. G. Wells, has been the basis for many movies. What Academy Award winner starred in the 1996 version?
ANS: MARLON BRANDO.

17) What comedian played a Shakespearean actor in "To Be or Not to Be?"
ANS: JACK BENNY.

18) What famous opera singer starred in only one motion picture, "Yes, Giorgio."
a) Ezio Pinza b) Robert Merrill c) Lauritz Melchior d) Luciano Pavarotti
ANS: D

19) Which popular singer of the 1950s co-starred in

the musical, "Kismet?"
a) Elvis Presley b) Vic Damone
c) Eddie Fisher d) Fabian
ANS: B

20) What is the name of Elvis Presley's first movie?
a) "Love Me Tender" b) "King Creole" c) "G.I. Blues" d) "Kid Galahad"
ANS: A

ELVIS PRESLEY

21) What was one of the unique elements about the 2011 film, "The Artist?"
ANS: IT WAS BASICALLY A SILENT MOVIE.

22) What was the title of non-musical version of "The King and I?"
ANS: "ANNA AND THE KING OF SIAM."

23) What city was the setting for "Bullitt" and its famous car chase?
ANS: SAN FRANCISCO.

24) What year is generally accepted as the first year a full length feature was shot digitally instead of on film?
a) 2001 b) 1987 c) 1998 d) 2010
ANS: B. THE MOVIE WAS "JULIA AND JULIA."

25) William Powell's career ran from 1922 to 1955. What was his final film?
a) "How to Marry a Millionaire" b) "The Girl Who Had Everything" c) "Mr. Roberts" d) "The Treasure of Lost Canyon"
ANS: C

26) How many "Harry Potter" films have been

made through 2016?
a) 8 b) 6 c) 9 d) 5
ANS: A

27) Who was the non-simian star of "Planet of the Apes?"
ANS: CHARLTON HESTON.

28) What opera has been the source for the most movie versions?
a) "La Boheme" b) "Carmen" c) "La Tosca"
d) "Aida"
ANS: B

29) Tom Cruise was a veteran of what war in "The Last Samurai?"
ANS: THE CIVIL WAR.

30) How many "James Bond" films have been made through 2016?
a) 21 b) 19 c) 22 d) 26
ANS: D

31) Who was Groucho Marx's straight woman in seven films?
a) Margaret Sullivan
b) Margaret Dumont c) Zasu Pitts d) Una Merkel
ANS: B

32) Who did producer Hal Wallis want to star with Elvis Presley in a cowboy movie?
a) Steve McQueen b) John Wayne c) Roy Rogers d) Alan Ladd
ANS: B

SARAH JESSICA PARKER

JANET GAYNOR

33) What film told the story of Olympic track star Lou Zamperini and his capture by the Japanese during World War II?
ANS: "UNBROKEN."

34) How many years have there been between the two "Birth of a Nation" films?
a) 99 b) 101 c) 100 d) 75
ANS: B

35) Lady Gaga is reportedly set to star in a 2018 remake of "A Star is Born." What actresses starred in the 1937, 1954 and 1976 versions of the film?
ANS: JANET GAYNOR, JUDY GARLAND AND BARBRA STREISAND.

36) What film had a computer named "Hal" in it?
ANS: "2001, A SPACE ODESSEY."

37) There have been innumerable versions of "The Three Musketeers" made as motion pictures. What year did the first version appear?
a) 1911 b) 1903 c) 1899 d) 1919
ANS: B

38) Basil Rathbone is well known for his portrayals of Sherlock Holmes in several films. What actor played Dr. Watson in these movies?
ANS: NIGEL BRUCE.

39) One of these actresses did not make a movie with Elvis Presley:
a) Barbara Stanwyck b) Angela Lansbury c) Nancy Sinatra d) Kathryn Grayson
ANS: D

40) Who was the female lead in the film version of "The Man from La Mancha?"
ANS: SOPHIA LOREN.

41) What 1961 musical was based on the Romeo and Juliet story?
ANS: "WEST SIDE STORY."

42) In one of his rare non-cowboy roles, what does John Wayne play in "Trouble Along the Way?"
a) A detective b) A coach c) A soldier b) An oil rigger
ANS: B

SYLVESTER
STALLONE

43) He gained fame for his role of Uncle Fester in the 1960s TV series, "The Addams Family," but much earlier he played the title role in the 1921 classic, "The Kid," opposite Charlie Chaplin. Who was he?
ANS: JACKIE COOGAN.

44) What year did the first "Star Wars" movie come out?
a) 1977 b) 1979 c) 1981 d) 1973
ANS: A

45) In what feature-length movie did Mickey Mouse have a role?
ANS: "FANTASIA." (1940)

46) What screen character has been played by the most different actors?
a) Superman b) Frankenstein's monster c) Batman d) The Lone Ranger
ANS: C. BATMAN (9).

CHARLIE CHAPLIN AND
JACKIE COOGAN IN
"THE KID," 1921.

47) Robert Alda played the lead on Broadway, Marlon Brando starred in the film version. What was the movie?
ANS: "GUYS AND DOLLS."

48) In what James Bond movie was "Oddjob" one of the villains?
ANS: "GOLDFINGER."

49) Doris Day and David Niven co-starred in what film?
ANS: "PLEASE DON'T EAT THE DAISIES" (1960).

50) In the 1966 remake of "Stagecoach," who played the role of Doc Boone, portrayed by Thomas Mitchell in the 1939 version?
a) Arthur Kennedy b) Thomas Mitchell c) Bing Crosby d) Van Heflin
ANS: C

51) Dizzy and Daffy are characters from what movie?
a) "Looney Tunes" b) "Meet Me in St. Louis" c) "The Pride of St. Louis" d) "Snow White and the Seven Dwarfs"
ANS: C (THEY WERE THE DEAN BROTHERS.)

52) What was the film in which James Stewart co-starred with an invisible rabbit?
ANS: "HARVEY."

53) In "Arsenic and Old Lace," the character por-trayed by Raymond Massey was written for and

played by whom on Broadway?
ANS: BORIS KARLOFF.

54) "Night and Day" is the title of the film, the name of a song in the film and the biography of the composer of the song. Who was he?
ANS: COLE PORTER.

55) In what film were Humphrey Bogart and William Holden brothers?
ANS: "SABRINA" (1954)

56) What was the first feature motion picture to be broadcast on prime-time television?
a) "King Kong" b) "Ben-Hur" c) "A Christmas Carol" d) "The Wizard of Oz."
ANS: D, IN 1956.

57) What actor lost the weekend in "The Lost Weekend?"
ANS: RAY MILLAND.

58) The first feature-length animated film cele-brated its 75th anniversary in 2012. What was it?
ANS: "SNOW WHITE AND THE SEVEN DWARFS."

59) What James Bond film was the first-ever to earn a bil-lion dollars worldwide?
a) "Goldfinger" b) "On Her Majesty's Secret Service" c) "Skyfall" d) "From Russia With Love"
ANS) C

60) True or False? "The Hunger Games" had the fourth largest

BETTY HUTTON

THE MOVIE GAME • The Movies

BETTE DAVIS AND
ERROL FLYNN IN
"THE PRIVATE LIVES OF
ELIZABETH AND ESSEX,"
1939.

opening weekend in movie history and the largest opening night box-office for a non-sequel in 2012.
ANS: TRUE.

61) The first Tarzan film was released in what year?
a) 1922 b) 1932 c) 1918 d) 1939
ANS: C

62) What was the last film made by The Beetles?
ANS: "LET IT BE" IN 1970.

63) James Stewart played Glen Miller in "The Glenn Miller Story" (1954). Who played Benny Goodman in "The Benny Goodman Story" (1956)?
a) Tony Curtis b) Steve Allen c) Danny Thomas d) Larry Parks
ANS: B

64) What was the first film to be based on a television series?
a) "MASH" b) "Bewitched" c) "Dragnet" d) "77 Sunset Strip"
ANS: C

65) Who played Mozart in the award-winning "Amadeus," 1984?
ANS: TOM HULCE.

66) Steve McQueen had his first starring role in what movie?
a) "The Wasp Woman" b) "Not of This Earth" c) "The Blob" d) "Attack of the Crab Monsters"
ANS: C

TOM HULCE
IN "AMADEUS"

67) Who played the Monster in "Young Frankenstein?"
ANS: PETER BOYLE.

68) In what film did James Cagney appear after a 20-year retirement?
ANS: "RAGTIME" IN 1981.

69) Because of poor returns at the box office and an extremely high budget, this film's name became synonymous with "flop."
a) "Annie" b) "Heaven's Gate" c) "Ishtar"
d) "Cleopatra"
ANS: B

70) What was Inspector Clouseau's first name in "The Pink Panther" movies?
a) Raoul b) Henri c) Louis d) Jacques
ANS: D

71)) What was the San Francisco stadium used for the climatic scene in "Dirty Harry?"
a) Candlestick Park b) Seals Stadium
c) Kezar Stadium d) AT&T Park
ANS: C

72) In the first of the Hardy family series, the 1937 film, "A Family Affair," Lionel Barrymore plays Judge Hardy. Who played the judge in subsequent

LINDA DARNELL

Hardy films?
a) Lewis Stone b) Charlie Grapewin c) Frank Morgan d) Leo G. Carroll
ANS: A

73) The 1939 film, "Swanee River" was the biography of what composer?
a) Al Jolson b) George M. Cohan c) Stephen C. Foster d) George Gershwin
ANS: C

74) The movie, "Pin Up Girl," (1944), starred Hollywood's most famous pin up girl of the time. Who was she?
a) Marilyn Monroe b) Alice Faye c) Rita Hayworth d) Betty Grable
ANS: D

75) When John Alexander, portraying "Teddy Roosevelt" Brewster in "Arsenic and Old Lace," runs up the stairs, what one-word line does he shout out?
a) Bully! b) Attack! c) Charge! d) Forward!
ANS: C

76) What make of car was used in the "Back to the Future" films?
a) Corvette b) DeLorean c) Maserati d) Mustang
ANS: B

PAULETTE GODDARD

77) These three movies were made in what year?
"The Godfather II," "Chinatown" and "Blazing Saddles."
a) 1974 b) 1976 c) 1977 d) 1972
ANS: A

78) In the movie of the same name, what is
"Excalibur?"
a) King Arthur's horse b) King Arthur's sword
c) King Arthur's shield d) King Arthur's castle
ANS: B

79) Betty Hutton starred as actress Pearl White in
a 1947 film based on a 1914 serial. What was the
film and the serial's title?
ANS: "THE PERILS OF PAULINE."

80) Set in Dogpatch and based on one of the country's favorite comic strips of the 1940s, this movie
was adaped from the Broadway musical. What was
it?
ANS: "LI'L ABNER."

JOEL MC CREA   RANDOLPH SCOTT

BASIL RATHBONE

81) Who played writer George Plimpton in "Paper Tiger?"
ANS: ALAN ALDA.

82) Joan Collins played her in the 1955 bio-film, "The Girl in the Red Velvet Swing." Who was she?
ANS: EVELYN NESBIT.

83) What was the badge number of Harry Callahan, played by Clint Eastwood, in "Dirty Harry?"
a) 714 b) 2121 c) 711 d) 2211
ANS: D

84) One of filmdom's all-time beauties, Ava Gardner, played the female lead in this 1951 film.
a) "Pandora and The Flying Dutchman" b) "David and Bathsheba" c) "Golden Girl" d) "The Ghost and Mrs. Muir"
ANS: A

AUDREY HEPBURN AND WILLIAM HOLDEN
IN "SABRINA," 1954.

85) Don Ameche was a co-owner and team president of the Los Angeles Dons and had a film career that began in 1936. But it wasn't until 1985 that he won a Best Supporting Actor Oscar for what film?
ANS: "COCOON."

86) In 1962, veteran actors Joel McCrea and Randolph Scott co-starred in a classic western near the end of their careers. What was it?
ANS: "RIDE THE HIGH COUNTRY."

87) She had her first major role in the 1936 film, "Modern Times," married her leading man (Charlie Chaplin) and was nominated for a best supporting actress Oscar in 1943 for her role in "So Proudly We Hail." Who was she?
ANS: PAULETTE GODDARD.

88) "Forever Amber" was a popular novel in 1944 that was turned into a movie in 1947. Who won the coveted role of Amber in the film?
a) Hedy Lamarr b) Gene Tierney c) Linda Darnell

EVELYN NESBIT   JOAN COLLINS

d) Jennifer Jones
ANS: C

89) Jean Arthur began her career in the silents, made three films for director Frank Capra and co-starred with Alan Ladd in her only color movie, in 1953. It was her final big screen appearance. What was the movie?
ANS: "SHANE."

90) Sylvester Stallone starred in "Rocky" in 1976. By the time "Creed" was released in 2016, how many sequels to the original film had been made?
a) 4 b) 8 c) 6 d) 5
ANS: C

MARGARET DUMONT

91) She and her husband, Matthew Broderick, had different movies premiering on the same day in 2005. His was "The Producers," hers was "The Family Stone." Who is she?
ANS: SARAH JESSICA PARKER.

92) He used his fencing skills to good advantage as the villain in such films as "The Adventures of Robin Hood" (1938) and "The Mark of Zorro" (1940). Who was he?
ANS: BASIL RATHBONE.

93) What was Bullitt's first name in the film of the same name, starring Steve McQueen?

ALAN LADD

ANS: FRANK.

94) The "Magnificent Seven" movie of 1960 was based on what film that was made in 1954?
ANS: "THE SEVEN SAMURAI."

95) How many "Ma and Pa Kettle" films were made between 1947 and 1957?
a) 5 b) 10 c) 6 d) 3
ANS: B

96) In the Marx Brothers comedy, "A Night at the Opera," what opera was it that was being performed?
a) "Otello" b) "Carmen" c) "I Pagliacci"
d) "Il Trovatore"
ANS: D

97) The first version of "Whistling in the Dark" was made in 1933 and starred Ernest Truex. A second version was made in 1941 and was followed by two sequels, in 1942 and 1943. Who starred in them as "The Red Fox?"

ETHEL BARRYMORE   LIONEL BARRYMORE

ANS: RED SKELTON.

98) In the 1949 film, "A Letter to Three Wives," who was the third wife besides Jeanne Crain and Linda Darnell?
a) Ann Blyth b) June Allyson c) Ann Sothern d) Jane Powell
ANS: C

99) Cliff Edwards sang "When You Wish Upon a Star" in what movie?
ANS: "PINOCCHIO."

JEANNE CRAIN

100) The eight-foot Wookie who first appeared in the initial "Star Wars" film was called?
ANS: CHEWBACCA.

101) Humphrey Bogart made three consecutive films with locations in the titles. Two were "Across the Pacific" in 1942 and "Action in the North Atlantic" in 1943. What was the one in the middle?
ANS: CASABLANCA.

102) The Barrymore siblings, John, Lionel and Ethel, appeared in only one movie together. What was it?
ANS: "RASPUTIN AND THE EMPRESS," IN 1932.

103) Who was "baby" in the 1938 film, "Bringing Up Baby"?

SUSAN HAYWARD

ANS: A PET LEOPARD.

104) Who was the voice of Baloo the Bear in the 1966 animated version of "The Jungle Book"?
a) Mel Blanc b) Phil Harris c) W. C. Fields d) Groucho Marx
ANS: B

VICTOR MATURE

105) In "Mr. Deeds Goes to Town," Gary Cooper had an unusual first name. What was it?
a) Herkimer b) Cosmo c) Longfellow d) Atticus
ANS: C

106) The Andy Hardy series at MGM ran from 1937 until 1946, then there was how long of a break before the next, and last, episode was released?
a) 10 years b) 5 years) c) 7 years d) 12 years
ANS: D (1958).

RED SKELTON

107) This gangster was first played by Wallace Berry in 1931 and by such actors as Paul Muni, Barry Sullivan, Jason Robards Jr. and Robert DeNiro. Who was he?
ANS: AL CAPONE.

108) Raffles, the gentleman burglar, was played in the movies by all but one of the following:
a) Ronald Colman b) Robert

ALEC GUINESS

Donat c) David Niven d) John Barrymore
ANS: B

109) "Demetrius and the Gladiators," 1954, starring Victor Mature and Susan Hayward, was the sequel to what film, made in 1953, that was based on a best-selling novel?
ANS: "THE ROBE."

110) What incident was it that Jack Lemmon and Tony Curtis witnessed that caused them to flee Chicago in "Some Like It Hot?" (1959).
ANS: THE ST. VALENTINE'S DAY MASSACRE.

111) She was reportedly the original choice for the Margo Channing role in the 1950 film, "All About Eve," but was dropped because she was too young.
a) Susan Hayward b) Claudette Colbert c) Olivia DeHavilland d) Rita Hayworth
ANS: A

112) Paul Muni was nominated for an Oscar for his first film appearance in "The Valiant" in 1929 and for his last film appearance in what 1959 movie?
ANS: "THE LAST ANGRY MAN."

113) True or False: Charles Boyer said, "Come with me to the Casbah" in "Algiers," 1938.
ANS: FALSE. THE LINE WAS NOT IN THE MOVIE.

PAUL MUNI

The Awards

1) What movie won the first Best Film Oscar?
ANS: "WINGS."

2) As of 2017, three films are tied with the most Academy Awards by a single film at 11. Can you name them?
ANS: "BEN-HUR" (1959), "TITANIC" (1997), "THE LORD OF THE RINGS: THE RETURN OF THE KING" (2003).

3) What are the most *nominations* received by a single film?
a) 12 b) 20 c) 14 d) 16
ANS: C

4) One of the following films did not receive a record number of nominations.
a) "The Godfather I b) "All About Eve" c) "Titanic"
d) "La La Land"
ANS: A

5) What male received the

BOB HOPE

most Academy Awards? (Hint — he was not an actor.)
ANS: WALT DISNEY WITH 22 OSCARS.

6) What female received the most Oscars. (Not an actress.)
ANS: COSTUME DESIGNER EDITH HEAD, EIGHT.

7) Who has won the most awards for Acting?
ANS: KATHARINE HEPBURN WITH FOUR, ALL FOR BEST ACTRESS.

8) What director has won the most awards?
ANS: JOHN FORD, WITH FOUR.

9) Shirley Booth, Julie Andrews, Barbra Streisand and Marlee Matlin all have one thing in common regarding the Academy Awards. What is it?
ANS: EACH WON AN OSCAR FOR THEIR FILM DEBUT ACTING PERFORMACES.

10) What film, oftentimes selected as the greatest movie of all times, did not win the Oscar as best picture the year of its release.
ANS: "CITIZEN KANE," 1941.

GREER GARSON

11) Oscars for Best Picture, Director, Actor, Actress and Screenplay are considered the Big Five Academy Awards. What one of the following was not a Big Five winner?
a) "It Happened One Night"
b) "Citizen Kane" c) "One Flew Over The Cuckoo's Nest"
d) "The Silence Of The Lambs."
ANS: B

12) What actors have won consecutive Oscars?
a) Marlon Brando and Tom Hanks. b) Spencer
Tracy and Richard Burton c) Tom Hanks and
Spencer Tracy.
ANS: C (TRACY FOR "CAPTAINS COURAGEOUS," 1937, AND
"BOYS TOWN," 1938 AND HANKS FOR "PHILADELPHIA," 1993
AND "FOREST GUMP," 1994.)

13) What actresses have won consecutive awards?
a) Katharine Hepburn and Sophia Loren b) Luise
Rainer and Claudette Colbert c) Katharine Hep-
burn and Luise Rainer
ANS: C (RAINER FOR "THE GREAT ZIEGFELD," 1936, AND "THE
GOOD EARTH," 1937, AND HEPBURN FOR "GUESS WHO'S
COMING TO DINNER," 1967 AND "THE LION IN WINTER,"
1968.)

14) Where were the first Academy Awards held, in
1929?
a) Pantages Theater b) Hollywood Roosevelt Hotel
c) Coconut Grove d) Shrine Auditorium
ANS: B

15) Who is the actor who won consecutive Best Sup-
porting actor awards?
ANS: JASON ROBARDS FOR "ALL
THE PRESIDENT'S MEN," 1976 AND
"JULIA," 1977.

16) What actresses have won
consecutive Oscars in the Best
Supporting Actress category?
ANS: THERE HAS BEEN NONE...SO
FAR.

17) Who is the first woman to
win a Best Director Oscar?
ANS: KATHRYN BIGELOW FOR "THE
HURT LOCKER" IN 2007.

HATTIE MC DANIEL

18) Who is the first actress to

WALTER BRENNAN

receive 10 nominations for acting?
a) Meyrl Streep b) Bette Davis
c) Katharine Hepburn
d) Janet Gaynor
ANS: B

19) Who was the youngest winner of an acting award?
ANS: TATUM O'NEAL WON BEST SUPPORTING ACTRESS IN "PAPER MOON" AT AGE 10 IN 1973.

20) Conversely, who is the oldest winner of an acting award?
ANS: CHRISTOPHER PLUMMER WON BEST SUPPORTING ACTOR AT AGE 82 FOR "BEGINNERS," 2011.

21) Clark Gable, Charles Laughton, Victor McLaglen and Franchot Tone were the nominees for Best Actor in the 1935 Academy Awards. Who won?
ANS: VICTOR McLAGLEN FOR "THE INFORMER."

22) What was similar about actors Robert Redford and Kevin Costner's winning Oscars for Directing?
ANS: BOTH WON AWARDS FOR THE FIRST FILM THEY DIRECTED.

23) Who was the first African-American performer to win an Academy Award?
ANS: HATTIE McDANIEL IN 1939 WON BEST SUPPORTING ACTRESS FOR "GONE WITH THE WIND."

24) Who directed the only Academy Award performances of both James Cagney and Joan Crawford?
ANS: MICHAEL CURTIZ.

25) What year did more than one African-American performer win an acting Oscar?

ANS: 2002. DENZEL WASHINGTON
WON BEST ACTOR FOR "TRAINING
DAY" AND HALLE BERRY WON BEST
ACTRESS FOR "MONSTER'S BALL."

26) This actor won Best Supporting Oscars three out of
five years but none was back
to back. Who was he?
a) Donald Crisp b) Walter
Brennan c) Barry Fitzgerald
d) Van Heflin
ANS: B

FRANCES MARION

27) Joseph L. Mankiewicz won
back-to-back Best Director Os-
cars in 1950 ("A Letter to Three
Wives") and 1951 ("All About Eve"). It wasn't until
what years another director repeated the fete.
What years and who was he?
ANS: ALEJANDRO G. INARRITU FOR "BIRDMAN" IN 2015 AND
"THE REVENANT" IN 2016.

28) Bette Davis was nominated for an Oscar 10
times. How many did she win?
ANS: 2, "DANGEROUS" IN 1935 AND "JEZEBEL" IN 1938.

29) The 1996 motion picture "Jerry Maguire" is con-
sidered to be Renee Zellweger's break-through film.
In what year did she win an Academy Award?
ANS: 2004 – BEST SUPPORTING ACTRESS FOR "COLD
MOUNTAIN."

30) Reese Witherspoon won an Academy Award for
best actress in what 2005 film?
ANS: "WALK THE LINE."

31) She received the first Best Actress Oscar in
1927, but said at the time she was more excited
about meeting Douglas Fairbanks.

ALEJANDRO
INNARUTU

ANS: JANET GAYNOR.

32) Michael Curtiz won an Academy Award as best director of what film?
a) "Yankee Doodle Dandy"
b) "The Adventures of Robin Hood" c) "Casablanca"
d) "Mildred Pierce"
ANS: C

33) A musical, "The Broadway Melody," won the Outstanding Picture Award at the 1929 Academy Awards. What was the next musical to win best picture and in what year?
ANS: "AN AMERICAN IN PARIS," 1952.

34) His running gag was that he was never even nominated for an Oscar, let alone winning one. But he emceed the Academy Awards program a record-setting 19 times. Who was he?
ANS: BOB HOPE.

35) Who was the youngest *nominee* for Best Director?
a) Norman Taurog b) Damien Chazelle c) John Singleton
d) Orson Welles
ANS: C. JOHN SINGLETON WAS 24 WHEN HE WAS NOMINATED FOR "BOYZ N THE HOOD," 1991.

36) Who was the youngest *winner* of Best Director?
a) Norman Taurog b) Damien Chazelle c) John Singleton
d) Orson Welles

JASON ROBARDS

ANS: B. CHAZELLE WAS 32 WHEN
HE WON IN 2017 FOR "LA LA LAND."

37) Who was the oldest *nomi-nee* for Best Director?
a) John Ford b) John Huston
c) Clint Eastwood d) Cecil B.
DeMille
ANS: B. HUSTON WAS 79 WHEN
NOMINATED FOR "PRIZZI'S HONOR"
IN 1985.

38) Who was the oldest *winner* for Best Director?
a) John Ford b) John Huston
c) Clint Eastwood d) Cecil B.
DeMille

VICTOR MC LAGLEN

ANS: C. EASTWOOD WAS 74 WHEN HE WON FOR "MILLION
DOLLAR BABY" IN 2004.

39) What was the longest on-screen performance to win an Acting Oscar?
a) 1 Hour, 23 Minutes b) 2 Hours, 23.5 Minutes c) 1 Hour 47.5 Minutes d) 2 Hours 11 Minutes
ANS: B, BY VIVIEN LEIGH IN "GONE WITH THE WIND," 1939.

40) What was the shortest on-screen performance to win an Acting Oscar?
a) 34 Minutes, 45 Seconds b) 1 Hour, 5 minutes
c) 19 Minutes 22 Seconds d) 5 Minutes, 2 Seconds
ANS: D. BEATRICE STRAIGHT IN "NETWORK," 1976.

41) What actress has had the most nominations?
a) Bette Davis b) Katharine Hepburn c) Meryl Streep d) Joan Crawford
ANS: C. MERYL STREEP HAS HAD 20 NOMINATIONS
THROUGH 2017.

42) What actor has had the most nominations?

HELEN HAYES

a) Marlon Brando b) Jack Nicholson c) Tom Hanks d) Laurence Olivier
ANS: B. JACK NICHOLSON HAS HAD 12 ACTING NOMINATIONS THROUGH 2017.

43) What African-American actor has won the most acting awards?
ANS: DENZEL WASHINGTON WITH 2,THROUGH 2017: BEST SUPPORTING ACTOR FOR "GLORY," 1989 AND BEST ACTOR FOR "TRAINING DAY," 2001.

44) What was unique about Barry Fitzgerald's nominations for 1944's "Going My Way?"
ANS: HE WAS NOMINATED FOR BEST ACTOR AND BEST SUPPORTING ACTOR FOR THE SAME ROLE.

45) How many decades has John Williams received a nomination?
a) 4 b) 3 c) 6 d) 5
ANS: C

46) Who are the only persons to win both an Oscar and Nobel Prize?
ANS: BOB DYLAN, AN OSCAR, 2000, A NOBEL, 2016. GEORGE BERNARD SHAW, OSCAR,1938, NOBEL, 1925.

47) Who is the only person to win an Oscar for Acting and Writing?
a) Orson Welles b) Emma Thompson c) Woody Allen d) Mel Brooks
ANS: B

GEORGE C. SCOTT

48) What was unique about the award Cate Blanchett won for Best Supporting Actress?
ANS: SHE PORTRAYED A REAL ACADEMY AWARD WINNER (KATHARINE HEPBURN) IN "THE AVIATOR."

49) What film series has won the most Best Picture awards?
ANS: "THE GODFATHER I" AND "THE GODFATHER II."

50) What director has had the most nominations?
a) Steven Spielberg b) Frank Capra c) John Ford d) William Wyler
ANS: D (12 NOMINATIONS).

51) What woman has had the most nominations?
a) Meryl Streep b) Edith Head c) Bette Davis d) Melissa Mathison
ANS: B. SHE HAD 35 NOMINATIONS.

52) What musical has won the most awards?
a) "Singin' in the Rain" b) "My Fair Lady" c) "Gigi" d) "West Side Story"
ANS: D

53) Who has had the most nominations for Best Original Screenplay?
a) William Goldman b) Orson Welles c) Woody Allen
d) Ernest Lehman
ANS: C. HE HAS HAD 16 NOMINATIONS, 3 WINS THROUIGH 2017.

54) Marlon Brando and Robert DeNiro won awards for playing the same character. Who was he?
ANS: VITO CORLEONE IN "THE GODFATHER I" AND "THE GODFATHER II."

55) What was the longest film

WALLACE BEERY

MYRNA LOY

to win the Best Picture award?
ANS: "GONE WITH THE WIND" AT 224 MINUTES.

56) What was the shortest film to win Best Picture?
ANS: "MARTY" AT 90 MINUTES.

57) Who gave the longest acceptance speech in Academy Awards history?
a) Bette Davis b) Kirk Douglas c) Greer Garson d) Meryl Streep
ANS: C. HER SPEECH RAN ALMOST SIX MINUTES.

58) What is the only tie for Best Actor in Oscar history?
ANS: WALLACE BERRY FOR "THE CHAMP" AND FREDRIC MARCH FOR "DR. JEKYLL AND MR. HYDE" IN 1932.

59) Why was "Limelight," released in 1952, not given an award until 20 years after its official release?
ANS: BECAUSE IT DID NOT PLAY IN LOS ANGELES COUNTY UNTIL 1972, A REQUIREMENT TO MAKE ANY FILM ELIGIBLE FOR AN AWARD.

60) What three actors have won awards for their portrayals of King Henry VIII of England?
ANS: CHARLES LAUGHTON, ROBERT SHAW AND RICHARD BURTON.

61) "Never on Sunday" won the award for best song in 1960. What language was it originally written in?
a) English b) Italian c) Greek d) Russian
ANS: C

62) He was the first person to win Academy Awards

CHRISTOPHER
PLUMMER

for producer, director and screenwriter of the same film. Who was he and what was the film?
ANS: BILLY WILDER FOR "THE APARTMENT" IN 1960.

63) Who was the first female to win an Oscar for Best Original Screenplay and for a non-acting achievement?
a) Edith Head b) Emma Thompson c) Frances Marion d) Betty Comden
ANS: C. FRANCES MARION (1930).

64) Which of these 1944 films was not nominated for best picture?
a) "Going My Way" b) "Laura" c) "Double Indemnity" d) "Wilson"
ANS: B

65) And the 2014 Best Picture winner is:
a) "Boyhood" b) "Birdman"
c) "American Sniper" d) "The Imitation Game"
ANS: B

66) The following all have what in common when it comes to Best Actor/Actress Academy Awards? Joseph Cotton, Errol Flynn, Edward G. Robinson, Myrna Loy, Fred Mac Murray, Maureen O'Hara.
ANS: THEY WERE NEVER NOMINATED FOR AN AWARD.

REESE
WITHERSPOON

BEATRICE STRAIGHT

67) Warren Beatty never won an acting Oscar but he did win one. What was it for?
ANS: BEST DIRECTOR, 1981.

68) Ernest Borgnine won the Oscar for Best Actor in 1955 for "Marty." Spencer Tracy was one of the best actor nominees that year — for a picture in which Borgnine appeared. What was that film?
A: "BAD DAY AT BLACK ROCK."

69) Who was the first actor to decline an Oscar nomination?
a) Marlon Brando b) George C. Scott c) Errol Flynn d) Robert De Niro
ANS: B. FOR "THE HUSTLER" IN 1961.

70) How long did Helen Hayes go between her Oscar wins for "The Sin of Madelon Claudet" and "Airport?"
a) 40 years b) 22 years c) 38 years d) 31 years
ANS: C. FROM 1932 TO 1970.

71) What was the first American film chosen as Best Picture at the Cannes Film Festival?
a) "Marty" b) "Some Like It Hot" c) "Quo Vadis" d) "Bonnie and Clyde"
ANS: A, IN 1955.

TATUM O'NEAL

72) She won a Best Supporting Actress Oscar in her feature film debut in "On the Waterfront" in 1954.
ANS: EVA MARIE SAINT.

73) How many actors won Academy Awards for their debut acting performance?
a) 1 b) None c)3 d) 2
ANS: B

74) What film won for Best Picture at the 1959 Academy Awards?
a) "Ben-Hur" b) "Anatomy of a Murder" c) "The Diary of Anne Frank" d) "Room at the Top"
ANS: A

HUMPHREY BOGART

75) The only Best Actress tie was in 1969 between what actresses?
ANS: KATHERINE HEPBURN ("A LION IN WINTER") AND BARBRA STREISAND ("FUNNY GIRL").

76) Humphrey Bogart won an Oscar for his role in which of the following films?
a) "The Caine Mutiny" b) "Key Largo"
c) "Casablanca" d) "The African Queen"
ANS: D

77) So what film did win the 2017 Best Picture Award?
a) "La La Land" b) "Manchester by the Sea"
c) "Fences" d) "Moonlighting"
ANS: D

The Movie Game

And yes, there is a "Movie Game." For the record, here is a detailed look at the game itself and how it is played.

THE GAME

Purpose

The purpose of the game is to earn more money than your opponent. The team with the most money at the end of the show will be the winner of the game and keeps the money it has won.

How the Game Is Played

The game is played between two teams. Each team is made up of a Player plus a Guest Celebrity. A Host will run the game.

To start the game, each Player will be introduced to the studio and home TV audience by the Host. Then the Host will bring out the two Guest Celebrities and introduce the Celebrities to their Player-teammates. Then the teams – Team One and Team Two – will take their places in the director's chairs in front of a console whose picture will also be visible on a large screen to the studio and home audience.

The game will be divided into four quarters. The 1st quarter has the easiest questions, the 4th, the hardest. Each team is staked to $5000 to start the game. For the first three quarters a team will draw $1000 to play the quarter. It will draw $2000 for the final, more difficult, quarter. Teams get 10 seconds to answer a question. A perfect answer in the first second earns the Team $1000. But, as the seconds tick down, the Team loses $100 per second. A correct answer earns $100 per second on the 10-second clock and, conversely, an incorrect answer loses $100 per second.

Team 1 starts the game with the first question, Team 2 gets the second question and questions then alternate back and forth between the two teams. Both teams will get an equal amount of questions during the game.

To start the Questions, the Host will ask Players on Team 1 to press the spinner button. Three question categories — similar to those which appear in this book — will immediately show on the screen and the Team will get to pick one category out of the three for its first question, which the Host will then proceed to ask.

The Player for Team 1 must punch a buzzer when he/she wants to answer. Only he/she can answer – not the Celebrity partner. Players, however, can and are encouraged to discuss the potential answer with the Celebrity partner. If they get the correct answer when the clock is at five seconds or $500, say, that money goes into their bank and on the scoreboard. If they are wrong, they get a minus $500.

After Team 1 plays out its question, Team 2 gets its try by picking a category after pressing the spinner button and then playing out that question.

A "Double Feature" question will pop up unexpectedly during the game. The Team that gets the double feature question will have the option of doubling its money on the next question. But it also will double its loss if it answers incorrectly, so it must decide to accept or not accept the "Double Feature" question.

Before the final round of questions, the Team in second place can challenge the Team in first place by requesting the Gauntlet question. The Team issuing the challenge must have money in the bank and must risk all the money it has won and if it fails to get the correct answer, its earnings go to zero. If the Team in second place does not want to issue a challenge it is allowed to keep the money it has won. No question category will be announced in advance of the Gauntlet challenge. It will be a general question from any category.

At the end of the game, Teams keep the money they have earned.

Game Notes

Question segments will be highlighted by visuals such as film clips of movie scenes, still photos, props and costumes, and audios such as movie music, star's voices, etc.

When the Host is introducing the guest Celebrities, the Celebrity's silhouette will appear on a large screen in the studio and after a brief bio is given of the Celebrity, he or she will step out and join the Host for a brief chit-chat before joining his teammate.

A Boy and Girl usher, dressed in typical usher costumes from the 30s, will walk the Celebrities and Players to their positions.

The Players and Celebrities will sit in director's chairs at a computer console on a very state-of-the-art set.

After reading a question, in order to give the Players a moment to think of an answer and win the top prize, the Host will say, "We're rolling...and...Action." The Player cannot push the answer button until after the word "Action" has been spoken by the Host. If he/she pushes it early, he/she loses the turn and the money that is on the board for that question.

When ending the show the Host will say, "That's a wrap...."

And a wrap it is.

ABOUT THE AUTHORS

Tony DiMarco and Tod Faulkner have been good friends since they worked together in the entertainment public relations field some years ago. DiMarco went on to become a television writer while Faulkner wrote free-lance articles for such publications as the Los Angeles Times, San Francisco Chronicle, Los Angeles Magazine and many others. He lives in the west San Fernando Valley. DiMarco lives in Los Angeles, just a few miles from Edendale, where the movie industry began in L.A.

Photos are from the authors' collection and Pixabay. Studio photos are from the Marc Wannamaker/Bison Archives.